ENHANCING SELF-ESTEEM & ACHIEVEMENT

A Handbook for Professionals

James Battle, PhD

SPECIAL CHILD PUBLICATIONS / SEATTLE

Special Child Publications
J. B. Preston, Editor & Publisher
P.O. Box 33548
Seattle, Washington 98133

Serving the special child since 1962

International Standard Book Number: 87562-076-0

91 90 89 88 87 86 85 84
10   9   8   7   6   5   4   3   2

ENHANCING SELF-ESTEEM & ACHIEVEMENT

I have learned during my brief life
That things worthwhile require sacrifice.
Children are worthy, capable, and significant:
With proper love and nurturance, they will grow up to be magnificent.

Children may be simple, complex, weak, or strong.
Their behavior may be shy, aggressive, right, or wrong.
Children are the most important sources of worth and life:
They are worthy of the love of mom, dad, husband and wife.

How parents handle children, determines what they will be,
How they see life, the world, you, and me.
Children's emotions are strong and true.
Teach them to love themselves, and they will love you.

—James Battle

Contents

The writer gratefully acknowledges the many individuals who have contributed to the development and publication of this book. First, I thank the many researchers using the *Culture-Free Self-Esteem Inventories for Children and Adults* who permitted me to list and cite findings from their research studies. Second, I gratefully acknowledge the Alberta Mental Health Advisory Council for providing funding for several of the studies reviewed in the book. Third, I thank the Department of Research of Edmonton Public Schools, for permitting me to conduct many of the studies that are reviewed in the book. Fourth, I gratefully acknowledge the assistance of the thousands of children and adults who participated in the studies that are cited in the book. Fifth, I thank Dorothy Battle, Edith Cary, and Rita Crawford for typing the manuscript. Finally, I dedicate this book to my wife Dorothy, and children Christina-Lynn and Jamie Alfred, for their patience and support during the many months it took to complete this project.

James Battle
March 1982

Preface

Although it is generally assumed that self-esteem is a major variable affecting achievement, little reliable data have been presented to support this position. This book is an attempt to summarize significant research findings dealing with the issue of self-esteem and achievement. In addition, this book offers practical methods of enhancing self-esteem and achievement.

The book is written in a fashion so that it can be readily understood by college students, teachers, and parents alike. We have attempted to provide a balance between scholarship and interest; and concerted effort was made to produce a book that would serve the diverse needs of these three reading audiences. There is a critical need for a book of this nature, because people concerned with education have recently realized that self-esteem and achievement are closely interrelated. More specifically, parents of children with learning problems have realized their children's self-esteem suffers as a consequence of learning difficulties. This realization is evident when one observes the growing number of requests for seminars dealing with the issue of self-esteem. For instance, in recent years I have conducted numerous workshops and seminars with professionals and laymen, and have found both groups to be keenly interested in the phenomenon of self-esteem, and particularly interested in the need to develop the affective component of children.

Authorities responsible for the implementation, development, and delivery of educational services, moreover, are realizing that teachers must attend to both cognitive and affective needs of developing children and youth in order to enable them to develop their potential to the fullest. For instance, recently the minister of education for a province in Northwestern Canada declared that his main objective for the 1980-81 school year was to facilitate the enhancement of the self-esteem of all pupils in his province. The board of trustees in the school system in which I am employed stated in its recent directive to the schools, that principals and teachers must make concerted efforts to "enhance the self-esteem of all pupils in their schools." The realization that self-esteem plays an important role in the learning process represents a new trend which may drastically affect our entire educational process, which has traditionally only attended to the cognitive aspects of the developing child. As a result of this new awareness, educators in current and future generations will be pressured by parents and other concerned groups to attend to and facilitate development of the affective aspects of the maturing child.

The book is unique in a number of ways. First, it is among the first to provide a comprehensive review of the phenomenon of self-esteem. Second, it provides a synthesis of self-esteem and achievement and describes how they interact and complement each other. Third, it incorporates a reference which summarizes 26 instruments used to assess self-regard. Fourth, it provides specific activities that have proven to be effective in enhancing self-esteem and achievement.

This book is organized in five parts:

Part I provides an introduction to the study of self-esteem. This section begins with an overview of the phenomenal self. It reviews some of the most commonly used definitions of the self and traces origins of the self.

Part II reviews some of the essential antecedents and major correlates of self-esteem.

Part III provides an analysis of the relationship between self-esteem and achievement. It also deals with the relationship between reading and self-esteem, an issue that has received considerable attention in recent years.

Part IV reviews scales intended to measure self-esteem, and specific activities that have proved to be of value in enhancing self-esteem and achievement are illustrated.

Part V provides an extensive reference list of research studies in the area of self-esteem. In addition, this section includes a subject index and an author index to the text.

I

THE PHENOMENAL SELF

ENHANCING

INTRODUCTION

The problem of academic underachievement has confronted psychologists and educators for generations, and numerous procedures and programs designed to facilitate achievement have been developed and implemented over the years. These techniques and programs, unfortunately, have been frequently ineffective and have often done little in modifying youngsters' achievement patterns. After many years of frustration, psychologists have started to explore the area of self-esteem for answers to this problem (underachievement) which continues to escalate. Many psychologists and most educators recognize that self-esteem and achievement are related. These two phenomena, in fact, are *highly* related, and, as a consequence, it is impossible to distinguish the two as completely separate entities. Our knowledge of the specific effects that each has on the other, however, is presently quite limited. We are currently in a stage of infancy in our understanding of the self-esteem/achievement process, and do not know how the two interact and complement each other. We do not know which occupies the foreground, and which occupies the background. Psychologists, moreover, have not been able to determine which of the two plays the antecedent and which follows. Is achievement motivation a consequence of positive self-esteem? Does academic success facilitate or enhance self-esteem? This book suggests answers to these and other pertinent questions. It explores the area of self-esteem and achievement and attempts to delineate clearly their antecedents and correlates. It offers synthesis of the relationship between the two, and presents specific means for enhancing achievement and self-esteem.

Our major thesis is that both self-esteem and achievement are essential variables in the educational process. Our approach to education, until quite recently, has tended to be one-sided; that is, we have concerned ourselves with achievement per se, but we have failed to inspect the "other side of the coin" and as a consequence have neglected almost completely the phenomenon of self-esteem. Remedial techniques especially, and educational programs in general, have often been ineffective in meeting the needs of our young people. Our inability to motivate young people to use their potential effectively is vividly reflected in the apathetic student, the underachiever, and the vast adolescent wasteland which provides refuge for so many North American youths.

The majority of these young people have experienced learning problems in school, which has a negative effect on their self-esteem. In addition, a large percentage of students with learning problems experience various forms of psychopathology. For instance, L. Yeudall (1977) studied incarcerated juvenile delinquents and found that 78 percent of them were experiencing learning disabilities, a condition associated with low self-esteem (Battle 1978, 1979; Battle and Blowers 1981). Also, a significant proportion of students with learning problems experience depression (Battle 1978, 1980). Depression in children and youth has increased significantly during the last decade, and suicide, which typically follows depression, is the second leading cause of death of North American youth of age six to nineteen. Although auto accidents are the leading cause of death of North American youngsters, most experts feel that many of the automobile fatalities are in reality self-induced. Psychologists, educators, and mental health workers generally agree that learning problems heavily tax the coping strategies of developing children and youth. Thus, learning problems tend to have a negative effect on pupils' perceptions of self-worth.

We have largely failed to incorporate procedures or techniques in our programs that are designed to enhance self-esteem. We nevertheless continue to expose youngsters to remedial programs (e.g., adaptation classes, resource rooms, individual tutoring) for long blocks of time without observing very much positive change. Many of these remedial approaches are sound in theory and methodology, but most fail to recognize the fact that we cannot change a person's achievement pattern until we modify the individual's perception of his ability to achieve. We propose that the development of an adequate sense of self should be a major goal of education. Research findings support the position just stated, and enlightened psychologists and educators generally agree that an adequate degree of self-esteem is essential for students because it affects their level of achievement, ability to adjust to the demands of enviroment, and general state of well being. Thus, if teachers are to become more effective in their attempts to develop their pupils' potential to the fullest and produce citizens who are capable of functioning productively in current and future generations, they must attend to the self-esteem needs of developing children and youth.

1

CHARACTERISTICS OF THE PHENOMENAL SELF

Phenomenologists, or "self-theorists," have made the most significant contributions in the study of the self. Phenomenologists stress subjective perception and propose that the individual reacts to the world in terms of his unique perception of it. Hence, perception is the most important variable determining behavior. The following case, that of Bob, illustrates the role that perception of self plays in behavior.

Case Report 1.1.

Bob was an average seventeen-year-old senior attending a small midwestern high school. Near the end of his senior year, Bob and other graduating seniors journeyed to the university to take college entrance examinations. Bob earned an average score on his examination, but a computer error assigned him a score at the 95th percentile. When Bob's test results reached the school, his principal was shocked to discover that Bob had earned the highest score in his school and was among the top two percent in the entire state. He found this particularly difficult to accept, because he and other faculty had always viewed Bob as being an average student. The principal, nevertheless, reassessed his perceptions of Bob and started to view him as being a very capable student. When the results were viewed by the counselor, he reassessed his perceptions of Bob, and assumed that the average standardized test scores Bob had earned throughout the years, apparently, were not valid indicators of his true level of potential. When Bob's results were observed by his home-room teacher, she reassessed her views of Bob. When she informed Bob's parents of his score, they started to view him differently.

After observing the way his principal, counselor, teacher, and parents were reacting toward him, Bob reassessed his perceptions of himself and started to see himself as not merely being "average" but quite capable. Subsequently, Bob became one of the highest achievers of his era. He is now a practicing physician.

Perception is the major determinant of behavior, and in most cases (as in the case of Bob) determines whether or not an individual makes significant or routine contributions to his society, because how we view ourselves determines how we respond to the demands of our environment. Phenomenologists state this position and argue that, regardless of how transformed or unconciously distorted an individual's perceptions may be, it is nevertheless his unique way of perceiving events which determines behavior. Phenomenologists, consequently, would argue that concepts and propositions must be formulated, not in terms of objective realities or unconcious processes, but instead in accordance with the way that events are conciously perceived by the individual. Phenomenologists also assume an individual's verbal statements accurately reflect his phenomenal reality. That is, one's verbal reports reveal the most basic and essential influences on his behavior. The phenomenological point of view is vividly illustrated in G. Kelly's (1970) paper describing his personal-construct theory, in which he states, "A person's processes are psychologically channelized by the ways in which he anticipated events." Kelly suggests that behavior is a private matter determined by our perceptions of events in the world.

Phenomenologists, therefore, attempt to observe behavior from the point of the individual, and assume that individuals behave according to reality as they themselves see it. An individual's behavior, therefore, may be considered to be irrelevant and irrational to the outsider, but, to the behaving individual, the behavior is relevant, purposeful, and pertinent to the situation as the individual understands it. The individual then, reacts to reality as it is seen by him and represented in his perceptual field. A. W. Snygg and D. Combs (1959) provide the following interpretation of the perceptual field.

> We shall use the concept (perceptual field) to refer to that more or less fluid organization of meanings existing for every individual at any instance. We call it the perceptual or phenomenal field. By the perceptual field, we mean the entire universe, including himself, as it is experienced by the individual at the instant of action. It is each individual's personal and unique field of awareness, the field of perception responsible for his every behavior (p. 20).

Behavior, according to Snygg and Combs, is determined totally by one's perceptual field. Their basic postulate, therefore, is that ". . . all behavior, without exception, is completely determined by, and pertinent to, the perceptual field of the behaving organism." Their position is consistent with the basic thesis of this book. Here, we will assume that perception is the major determinant of behavior. Subjective perception, not objective reality, determines the individual's characteristic reactions and behaviors. Take, for example, the case of the individual whose perceptions are distorted to the degree that they are grossly incongruent with reality. Regardless of how incongruent his perceptions are with objective reality, nevertheless, they will in every instance determine his behavior. The capable person who demeans himself is as counterproductive, and his behavior is as self-defeating, as that of the noncapable or poorly equipped person who demeans himself to the same extent. This line of reasoning is consistent with that of phenomenologists who hold that "reality" does not lie in the event, but rather in the phenomenon, that is, the individual's experience of the event. The perceptual field, according to phenomenologists, therefore, is the universe of naive experience of the individual, the daily interactions of the self and its environment, which each individual perceives as reality. The perceptual or phenomenal field, thus, is reality—the only reality the individual can know.

Although reality is a subjectively perceived experience, perceived reality does not necessarily determine what is appropriate or inappropriate for the individual or society. For instance, the perceived reality of a paranoid schizophrenic may be that he is "Jesus Christ" who can walk on water. Attempting to walk on water on the high seas probably isn't the most appropriate behavior for the person; likewise, if a person considers himself to be "God" (e.g., Reverend James Jones, notorious for the People's Temple disaster in Guyana), and convinces his followers that they should commit suicide, this form of behavior is obviously self-defeating and counterproductive for the individuals involved and society in general. Also, if a person perceives that he and his group are racially superior (e.g., Adolph Hitler), and as a result should persecute or dominate others, this is detrimental to the world community.

Characteristics of the Phenomenal Field

Snygg and Combs (1959) state that the phenomenal field is fluid and has stability and direction:

1. *The perceptual field is fluid.* The perceptual field is continually changing, and it is this fluidity which makes change in behavior possible. This fluidity, which permits the individual to adjust to or accommodate environmental demands, enables him to gratify specific needs. This capacity for change also makes possible the processes of learning, reasoning, remembering, forgetting, and creativity.
2. *The perceptual field has stability.* The perceptual field, although fluid, maintains a certain degree of organization and stability. A certain degree of organization is needed in order for the individual to adjust to the demands of his environment. Without a certain degree of stability, life would be hectic, haphazard, confused, and disoriented. With stability we have order and structure, which enable us to live effective lives.
3. *The perceptual field has direction.* The perceptual fields of different individuals differ when exposed to the same stimuli, and the perceptual field of a given individual tends to change somewhat when exposed to successive presentations of the same physical stimuli, but in spite of his changeability, maintains direction. Consequently, it is always organized and meaningful. Our perceptions are never merely masses of unrelated stimuli. We always perceive a total—a gestalt or configuration—never mere isolated stimuli.

The reader should note that Snygg and Combs' position is theoretical, and, like most theoretical propositions, it is not well anchored with quantitative data to support the hypotheses derived from the theory. Like all theories of personality, it leaves much to be desired in the way of scientific proof. In spite of these limitations, however, the position which assumes that perception is the major determinant of behavior is, in our opinion, a valid one.

Carl Rogers, the leading proponent of the school of phenomenology, likewise stresses the importance of the perceptual field, and postulates that every individual is the center of his changing world of experiences. Experiences, therefore, according to Rogers, must be viewed only in terms of their relevance to the individual. Rogers (1959) states that, as the individual matures, a portion of his experience is differentiated into a conscious perception of self-as-object, which he calls the self-concept. The self-concept, once formed, influences the perceptions, thoughts, and memories of the individual.

Rogers, who is felt by many to be the leading American exponent of "self-theory," presents the following postulates, which are intended to delineate his theory of personality:

1. *Postulated characteristics of the human infant.* Rogers postulates that the human organism, during the period of infancy, possesses the following attributes:

   a. He perceives his experience as reality. His experience is his reality. As a consequence, he has greater potential awareness of what reality is for him than does anyone else, since no one else can completely assume his internal frame of reference.

   b. He has an inherent tendency toward actualization of his organism.

   c. He interacts with reality in terms of his basic actualizing tendency. Thus, his behavior is the goal-directed attempt of the organism to satisfy the experienced need for actualization in the reality as perceived.

   d. In this interaction he behaves as an organized whole, as a gestalt.

   e. He engages in an organismic valuing process, valuing experience with reference to the actualizing tendency as a criterion. Experiences which are perceived as maintaining or enhancing the organism are valued positively. Those which are perceived as negating such maintenance or enhancement are valued negatively.

   f. He behaves with advice toward positively valued experiences and with adience toward those negatively valued.

2. *The development of self.*

   a. In line with the tendency toward differentiation, which is a part of the actualizing tendency, a portion of the individual's experience becomes differentiated and symbolized in an awareness of being, an awareness of functioning. Such awareness may be described as self-experience.

   b. This representation of awareness of being and functioning becomes elaborated, through interaction with the environment composed of significant others, into a concept of self, a perpetual object in his experiential field.

3. *The need for positive regard.*

   a. As the awareness of self emerges, the individual develops a need for positive regard. This need is universal in human beings, and in the individual, is persuasive and persistent. Whether it is an inherent or learned need is irrelevant to the theory, but Standal, who formulated the concept, regards it as the latter.

      (1) The satisfaction of this need is necessarily based upon inferences regarding the experiential field of another.

         (a) Consequently, it is often ambiguous.

      (2) It is associated with a very wide range of the individual's experiences.

      (3) It is reciprocal, in that, when an individual discriminates himself as satisfying another's need for positive regard, he necessarily experiences satisfaction for his own need for positive regard.

         (a) Hence, it is rewarding both to satisfy his need in another, and to experience the satisfaction of one's own need by another.

      (4) It is potent, in that the positive regard of any social order is com-

municated to the total regard complex which the individual associates with that social order.

   (a) Consequently, the expression of positive regard by a significant social other can become more compelling than the organismic valuing process, and the individual becomes more adient to the positive regard of such others than toward experiences which are of positive value in actualizing the organism.

4. *The development of the need for self-regard.*

   a. The positive regard satisfactions or frustrations associated with any particular self-experience or group of self-experiences, come to be experienced by the individual independently of positive regard transactions with social others. Positive regard experienced in this fashion is termed self-regard.

   b. A need for self-regard develops as a learned need developing out of the association of self-experiences with the satisfaction or frustration of the need for positive regard.

   c. The individual thus comes to experience positive regard or loss of positive regard independently of transactions with any social other. He becomes, in a sense, his own significant social other.

   d. Like positive regard, self-regard—which is experienced in relation to any particular self-experience or group of self-experiences—is communicated to the total self-regard complex.

5. *The development of conditions of worth.*

   a. When self-experiences of the individual are discriminated by significant others as being more or less worthy of positive regard, then self-regard becomes similarly selective.

   b. When a self-experience is avoided (or sought) solely because it is less (or more) worthy of self-regard, the individual is said to have acquired a condition of worth.

   c. If an individual should experience only unconditional positive regard, then no conditions of worth would develop, self-regard would be unconditioned, the needs for positive regard and self-regard would never be at variance with organismic evaluation, and the individual would continue to be psychologically adjusted, and would be fully functioning. This chain of events is hypothetically possible, and hence important theoretically, though it does not appear to occur in actuality.

6. *The development of incongruence between self and experience.*

   a. Because of the need for self-regard, the individual perceives his experience selectively, in terms of the conditions of worth which have come to exist in him.

      (1) Experiences which are in accord with his conditions of worth are perceived and symbolized accurately in awareness.

      (2) Experiences which run contrary to the conditions of worth are perceived selectively and distorted in accord with the conditions of worth, or are partly or wholly denied to awareness.

   b. Consequently, some experiences now occur in the organism which are not recognized as self-experiences, are not accurately symbolized, and are not organized into the self-structure in accurately symbolized form.

   c. Thus, from the time of the first selective perception in terms of conditions of worth, the states of incongruence between self and experience, of psychological maladjustment, and of vulnerability, exist to some degree.

7. *The development of discrepancies in behavior.*
   a. As a consequence of the incongruence between self and experience described in item 6, a similar incongruence arises in the behavior of the individual.
      (1) Some behaviors are consistent with the self-concept and maintain, actualize, and enhance it.
         (a) Such behaviors are accurately symbolized in awareness.
      (2) Some behaviors maintain, enhance, and actualize those aspects of the experience of the organism which are not assimilated into the self-structure.
         (a) These experiences are either unrecognized as self-experiences, or are perceived in distorted and selective fashion in such a way as to be congruent with self.

8. *The experience of threat and the process of defense.*
   a. As the organism continues to experience, an experience which is incongruent with the self-structure (and its incorporated conditions of worth) is perceived as threatening.
   b. The essential nature of the threat is that, if the experience were accurately symbolized in awareness, the self-concept would no longer be a consistent gestalt, the conditions of worth would be violated, and the need for self-regard would be frustrated; a state of anxiety would exist.
   c. The process of defense is the reaction which prevents these events from occurring.
      (1) This process consists of the selective perceptions or distortions of the experience and/or the denial to awareness of the experience or some portion thereof, thus keeping the total perception of the experience consistent with the individual self-structure and consistent with his conditions of worth.
   d. The general consequences of the process of defense, aside from its perseveration of the foregoing consistencies, are a rigidity of perception (due to the necessity of distorting perceptions), an inaccurate perception of reality (due to distortion and omission of data), and intensionability.*

Summary

Phenomenologists stress the role of subjective perception and assume that it is the most important determinant of behavior.

Carl Rogers, the main spokesman for the phenomenological orientation in North America, assumes that the human organism possesses an inherent motivational system which, by way of feedback, enables him to gratify his emotional needs. Rogers makes the

*From "A Theory of Therapy, Personality, and Interpersonal Relations as Developed in the Client-Centered Framework." In *Psychology: A Study of a Science*, ed. S. Koch, vol. 3, pp. 221-231. New York: McGraw-Hill. Copyright 1959. Used by permission of McGraw-Hill Book Company.

point that it is the individual's perception of his environment, not the objective reality of circumstances, which is most important to the behaving organism. Take, for example, the case of a child who is held by a friendly and affectionate person, but perceives this experience as being strange and frightening. The child, consequently, will react or respond to this experience by displaying anxiety and fear. Thus, it is the child's perception of the experience, not the reality of the situation, which determines his behavior. The reality which influences behavior is in every instance the *perceived* reality.

Rogers postulates that a portion of the individual's experience is differentiated into the self as the organism strives for actualization, and this differentiation subsequently materializes as a need for self-regard. This particular sequence (differentiation/striving for actualization) is very important in personality development. Consider, for example, the infant who learns to need love and finds the experience of love to be very satisfying, but does not know if he is receiving love or not. In order to gain this awareness (i.e., that he is receiving love), he has to observe his mother's face, gestures, and other ambiguous signs. From this observation he develops a total, a gestalt, of how he is regarded by his mother, and each new experience of love or rejection alters the gestalt until, finally, each behavior on his mother's part (e.g., disapproval of a specific behavior) tends to be experienced in a similar fashion (e.g., disapproval in general). This particular phenomenon is of utmost importance because it holds that the infant's behavior, as a consequence of this interaction with mother, tends to be influenced much more by maternal love than by concerns for maintenance and enhancement of the organism. The final "product," therefore, is the individual who learns to view himself basically in the same fashion that his mother views him. Consequently, some behaviors are not actually experienced organismically as satisfying; and other behaviors are regarded negatively when they are not actually experienced as unsatisfying. The individual's self-esteem, thus, is influenced basically by early experiences with significant other people (usually parents). When the individual behaves in accordance with these introjected values, which he takes from parents or parent surrogates, he has acquired conditions of worth, which implies that he cannot regard himself positively (i.e., having worth) unless he lives in terms of these introjected conditions.

The individual, as a consequence of his acquired conditions of worth, tends to distort perceptions that are incongruous with his established conditions of worth. Those experiences which are incongruent with one's conditions of worth are threatening to the self and cause disturbances within one's system. The person, therefore, becomes highly motivated to reduce this tension and attempts to eradicate it—either by distorting perception or by employing defensive maneuvers which prevent the experience from emerging into awareness.

The employment of defenses (unconscious processes which defend against anxiety) is the most common method used by individuals in their attempts to rid themselves of anxiety. Defenses, although protective, tend to deny, falsify, or distort reality and—as a consequence—are basically maladaptive.

Rogers views this phenomenon as being the basic dilemma of the human species, which is also the essential factor in self-estrangement—manifested by and characteristic of "man who is not true to himself." The individual experiencing self-estrangement refuses to display his own natural valuing ability, and insists on preserving the positive regard of others to such an extent that he is compelled to falsify some of the values he experiences, and to perceive them only in ways that reflect their value to others.

2

ANALYSIS OF THE SELF

The Self Defined

Before we begin our discussion of the origins of the self, it is essential that we first define the construct of self. This chapter, therefore, will deal exclusively with defining self-concept and self-esteem. We will discuss the origins of self in Chapter 3. Defining the self is by no means an easy task, because conceptual and operational definitions of the self vary significantly. With this in view, we take the construct "self-esteem" to mean different things to different individuals. Investigators intensify this problem even further, as a result of their insistence on defining the self in accordance with the demands of their particular design.

Phenomenologists, as a group, probably have directed greater energies toward study and exploration of the phenomenon of self than most others. As a result, the definitions that follow are basically phenomenological in nature. Most theorists see the self as being representative of the individual's perception of himself. One's perception of self is generally thought to influence the way he behaves, and his actions, in turn, are thought to influence the way he perceives himself. Phenomenologists also generally agree that self-perceptions emerge as a result of an individual's experience with his environment. There is also considerable consensus concerning the subjective aspect of the self. This assumed subjectivity leads psychologists to postulate that the self may be inferred, but not observed directly. Psychologists, furthermore, assume that self-esteem is multifaceted and differentiate between the self-concept per se and the *inferred* self-concept (Coopersmith 1967; Piers and Harris 1964; Battle 1981; Purkey 1970; and Sears and Sherman 1964). Additional support for this position is provided by A. W. Combs, D. W. Soper, and C. C. Courson (1963), who state that the self-concept is restricted to the individual's report of self, whereas the inferred self-concept is another individual's attribution of one's self-concept.

At this point an additional distinction must be made between the self-concept and the construct self-esteem. Many educators, unfortunately, tend to use the terms interchangably. The two constructs, although closely related, nevertheless refer to different aspects of the self. Support for this position is provided by S. Coopersmith (1967), who defines self-concept as:

> ... the totality of perceptions a person has about himself which are most vital to the individual himself and that seem to that individual to be "me" at all times and places.

Coopersmith in the same manuscript defines self-esteem as:

> ... the evaluation which the individual makes and customarily maintains with regard to himself. It expresses an attitude of approval or disapproval and indicates the extent to which the individual believes in himself to be capable, significant, successful, and worthy.

Additional support for differentiation of the constructs self-concept and self-esteem is provided by R. Wylie (1961) in her classic manuscript entitled *The Self-Concept*, in which she states that the self-concept is composed of a number of metadimensions, which include clarity, abstraction, refinement, certainty, stability, realism, and self-esteem.

Self-esteem, although felt to be more specific than self-concept, is nevertheless multifaceted. For instance, Coopersmith (1967) and I both state that self-esteem is composed of the following components: general self, social self/peers, school/academics, and home/parents.

The general consensus of phenomenologists is that the self is a multifaceted phenomenon which is comprised of a number of components that may be studied individually or collectively. This position is vividly illustrated by R. J. Shavelson, J. J. Hubner, and G. C. Stanton (1976), who state that the self-concept may be described as being: (1) organized, (2) multifaceted, (3) hierarchical, (4) stable, (5) developmental, (6) evaluative, and (7) differentiable.

Organized

The position that self-concept is an organized unit is based on the assumption that the individual's experience constitutes the data on which he bases his perceptions of self. The position holds that the human organism, in its attempt to reduce the complexity which its experiences demand, modifies or recodes them (experiences) in a simpler, less complex form by placing them in categories. Categorization simplifies the use of data received from experiences, and consequently enables the individual to function more efficiently. The particular categorical system adopted by the individual is determined by his cognitive processes and is a reflection of his particular culture. For example, if the child's experiences in general revolve around family, friends, and school, one would probably find upon investigation the categories of family, friends, and school in the child's descriptive statements about himself. The categories employed by the individual, therefore, are representative of the person's way of organizing experiences and giving them meaning.

Multifaceted

Many theorists (e.g., Battle 1976; Coopersmith 1967) assume that self is multifaceted. That is, they feel that it is not a unitarian phenomena, but rather is composed of a number of interrelated facets. Other supporters of this position include A. T. Jersild (1952) and P. S. Sears (1963) who include the dimensions of school, social acceptance, physical attractiveness, and ability in their self-esteem inventory. Coopersmith (1967) and I (1976) both state that self-esteem includes a general dimension as well as social, school, and parental dimensions. The general dimension involves an overall or general view of one's perception of his own worth; the social dimension refers to the individual's perception of interpersonal peer relationships; the school (academic) component refers to the individual's perception of his ability to succeed academically; the parental (home) dimension refers to the individual's perception of his status at home which includes his subjective perception of how he feels his parents view him.

Hierarchical

This aspect of the self delineates quite clearly that the self-concept, although general in nature, may be composed of various sub- or mini-components which may be ranked or ordered in a hierarchial fashion. Self-concept, thus, may be comprised of a hierarchy which may range from the individual's experiences in a particular situation (which may occupy the base) to general self-concept at its apex. Jersild's (1952) representation of such a hierarchy is presented in Figure 2.1.

The data presented in Figure 2.1 indicate that general self-concept, which occupies the apex of the hierarchy, may be divided into two components: academic and nonacademic components, and these components may be further divided into mini- or subcomponents. For instance, the academic component may be divided into subject-matter areas (e.g., English, History, Science, Math). This subcomponent (academic subject matter) may be further divided into specific areas within a given subject-matter area (e.g., grammar or composition in English). The nonacademic component, likewise, may be divided into social, emotional, and physical areas. These areas can subsequently be further divided into subareas (e.g., peers, emotional states, and physical appearance).

Stability

The self-concept (especially, general self-concept) tends to be stable and fairly resistant to change. The self-concept, thus, once established and differentiated, tends to be highly resistant to change. Consequently, we find high correlations between an individual's self-esteem when it is examined from time to time over the years. For instance, Coopersmith (1967) found a correlation coefficient of .70 between the pre- and posttest scores of 52 public school students for a three-year period; and I (1977) found a correlation of .74 for 33 grade-six students over a two-year period.

Developmental

A number of theorists (e.g., Engel 1959; Sears and Sherman 1964) assume that the self-concept is developmental in nature. These writers argue that youngsters acquire a self-concept as they develop in a fashion which is similar to the way they acquire a personality. Proponents of this position argue that neonates and young infants do not differentiate themselves from their environment, but acquire this ability gradually and, with

FIGURE 2.1. *One Possible Representation of the Hierarchic Organization of Self-Concept.*

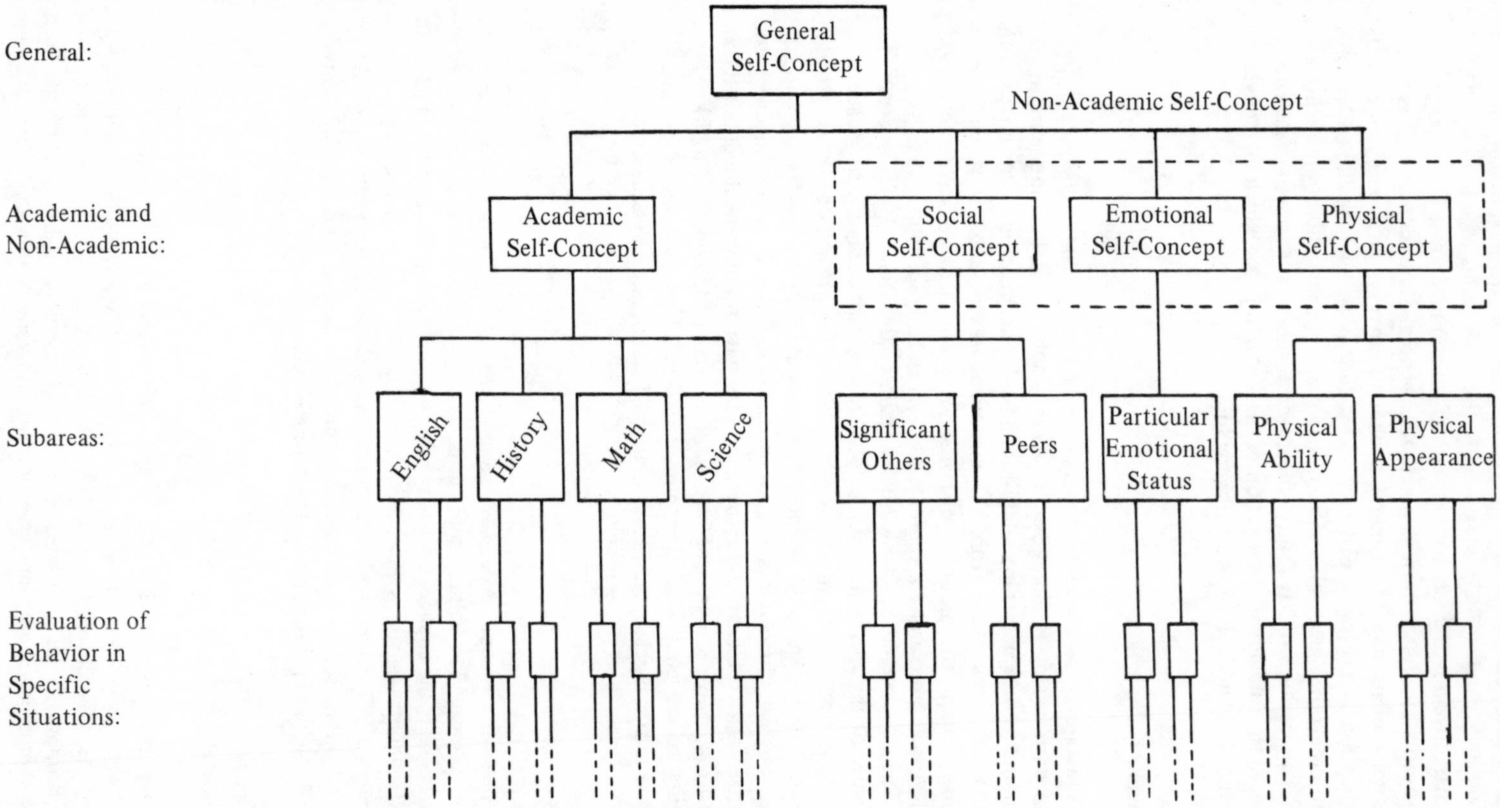

General:

Academic and
Non-Academic:

Subareas:

Evaluation of
Behavior in
Specific
Situations:

Source: Jersild, A. T. 1952. *In search of self.* New York: Teachers College Bureau of Publications.

maturity, become capable of distinguishing the self from the environment, objects, and others. The self-concept then, according to this position, becomes increasingly more differentiated with age until maturity.

Evaluative

The self-concept also includes an evaluative component which holds that the individual as he matures learns to evaluate his performance (e.g., actions, behaviors) in various situations and in response to different stimulus-objects.

The person, therefore, according to this line of reasoning, evaluates himself in relation to peers, parents, academically, etc. He also tends to evaluate himself in accordance to an ideal which is dictated by his superego. Take for example, the case of the individual who feels that he has to be flawless in order to be worthy of a positive self-evaluation. The individual who evaluates his performance with this standard, thus, would tend to perceive himself "negatively" if his performance is in any way less than perfect. For example, a youngster may be earning Bs—which satifies his teacher and parents, but may feel "dumb" because personally he feels he should earn As.

The individual, however, who insists that he must perform perfectly, is behaving in a counterproductive, pathological fashion, because perfection in personality functioning is an ideal that can never be actually experienced. The individual who feels that he must be perfect in order to be worthy, therefore, is doomed to continued episodes of failure, because he has put himself in a "Catch 22" type of situation, which can result in severe, negative consequences. For example, several years ago I provided psychotherapy for an eight-year-old boy who was achieving poorly. During my discussions with the child's mother, it became apparent that this boy's underachievement was his way of dealing with the hostility he possessed toward his mother, who insisted that he behave perfectly and earn perfect grades. "Catch-22": No matter how hard he tried, it was impossible for him to please his mother. Thus, he developed a tremendous amount of hostility for her which he could not express directly, but was able to express indirectly in underachievement. If he had permitted this profound degree of hostility to envelop his ego, seriously impeding its ability to function, he would have developed depression, which may have resulted in suicide. Suicide was not uncommon in this family. Three members, all males, had commited suicide during the middle-age mother's lifetime. The most recent suicide was the child's mother's brother, who shot himself after he completed a final examination that he apparently did not feel he did well on. He killed himself although he was maintaining a B average; and, of course, he did not see his final grade.

The differential associated with the evaluative component between individuals tends to be fairly variable and appears to be highly associated with one's cultural background. For instance, children reared in cultures where academic success is encouraged highly, will tend to evaluate their academic performance stringently. Children reared in cultures where physical poweress is most desirable or highly encouraged, will tend to emphasize and place higher values of worth on physical development than on academic success.

Differentiable

The self-concept is also felt to be differentiable from other self-constructs, although it may be related to them theoretically. Self-theorists, thus, generally agree that self-concept, although closely related to the personality in general, is nonetheless different, and as a consequence, can be differentiated from it. We believe, moreover, that there are differences between the various components of the self-concept—for example, between the academic self-concept and the nonacademic self-concept.

Self-Concept Defined

Although the constructs self-concept and self-esteem are generally used interchangeably, I am of the opinion that they refer to somewhat different phenomena; and as a result, I feel that appropriate distinctions should be made. Hence, definitions of self-concept and self-esteem will be presented separately.

Rogers (1951) offers the following definition of self-concept:

> The self-concept or self-structure may be thought of as an organized configuration of perceptions of the self which are admissable to awareness. It is composed of such elements as the perceptions of one's characteristics and abilities; the percepts and concepts of the self in relation to others and to the environments; the value qualities which are perceived as associated with experiences and objects; and goals and ideals which are perceived as having positive or negative value (p. 136).

Byrne (1974) offers the following definition:

> The self-concept may be defined simply as the total collection of attitudes, judgments, and values which an individual holds with respect to his behavior, his ability, his body, his worth as a person, in short, how he perceives and evaluates himself (p. 271).

Muller and Leonetti (1974) define the self-concept accordingly:

> The self-concept is the self-description the individual provides of himself (p. 5).

Although the definitions listed above differ slightly, their similarities outweigh observed differences. They all indicate that the self-concept is comprised of more than one dimension and that it possesses perceptual and evaluative components as well.

Self-Esteem Defined

N. Branden (1969), in his manuscript entitled *The Psychology of Self-Esteem*, states that self-esteem refers to:

> . . . an individual's view of himself. Self-esteem has two interrelated aspects. It entails a sense of personal efficacy and a sense of personal worth. It is the integrated sum of self-confidence and self-respect. It is the conviction that one is competent to live and worthy of living (p. 110).

In another publication (1981) I myself state that:

> Self-esteem refers to the perception the individual possesses of his own worth. An individual's perception of self develops gradually and becomes more differentiated as he matures and interacts with significant others. Perception of self-worth, once established, tends to be fairly stable and resistant to change (p. 14).

The definitions of self-esteem, like those of the self-concept, are all somewhat different, but are similar in many aspects. All definitions indicate that self-esteem is a subjective, evaluative phenomenon which determines the individual's characteristic perception of personal worth. Self-esteem develops gradually as the child interacts with significant others and becomes more differentiated with age.

Summary

Phenomenologists, who emphasize the role of perception, have offered numerous definitions of the self. Although the definitions tend to differ, there is fairly substantial agreement among them all. For instance, they generally agree that the self is a subjective, multifaceted phenomenon which develops gradually and is influenced significantly by early interactions with significant others.

Most psychologists, and educators, tend to use the constructs self-concept and self-esteem interchangeably; but distinctions should be made between the two. The self-concept represents a totality of one's perceptions, whereas self-esteem is one dimension of this "totality." Both self-esteem and self-concept are felt to be subjective phenomena which determine the individual's characteristic perception of himself.

ENHANCING

3

ORIGINS OF THE SELF

The self emerges and takes shape as the child develops and interacts with significant others. Although it is present at birth, it begins to develop in infancy when the youngster discovers himself as being a distinct individual and continues to develop throughout childhood as the individual becomes increasingly more aware of his physical image and various abilities. The self initially is a vague, poorly integrated, somewhat fragmented phenomenon, but becomes increasingly more different and integrated as the youngster matures. The self, therefore, represents the culmination of one's inherent make up and life experiences. The self, according to William James (1890), is the "sum-total of all that a person can call his." It is, thus, a composite of an individual's feelings, hopes, fears, thoughts, and views of who he is, what he is, what he has been, and what he might become.

A. T. Jersild (1960) states that the self is comprised of three interrelated components: perceptual, conceptual, and attitudinal.

Perceptual Component

The perceptual component refers to the characteristic way or ways that the individual perceives himself. It refers to the person's perception of personal worth, body image, and also includes the individual's perception of how he feels others view him. The individual's perception of self is determined by his early experiences and is influenced greatly by significant others. For instance, if the youngster feels that his parents view him as being worthy, he will subsequently view himself positively and worthy; conversely, if the youngster feels that his parents do not think highly of him, he will, likewise, view himself in a negative fashion. One's successes, in addition to impressions received from significant others, are a major force in shaping one's perception of personal worth. For instance, James (1890) states that perceptions of self depend entirely on what we think ourselves to be or do. Self-perception, according to James, is determined by the ratio of our supposed potentialities: a fraction in which our pretensions are the denominator; and the numerator, our success. Thus:

$$\text{self-esteem} = \frac{\text{success}}{\text{pretensions}}$$

Conceptual Component

The conceptual component of self refers to an individual's conception of his distinctive characteristics, abilities, and limitations. The conceptual component is cognitive and conative and refers to perceiving, knowing, and thinking, as well as acting, doing, willing, striving. The conceptual component also indicates one's conceptions of his origins, background, and outlook for the future.

Attitudinal Component

The attitudinal component of the self refers to the feelings the individual possesses of himself—for example, his beliefs, convictions, ideals, values, aspirations. The attitudinal component possesses evaluative, affective (feeling), and conative (action) aspects. The attitudinal component, according to Jersild (1960), includes the individual's attitudes, his tendency to view himself positively or negatively, and his convictions concerning his worthiness or unworthiness.

Development

The self develops gradually as the child matures, and becomes fairly stable about age ten. It is present at birth, commences development during the first year of life, and becomes more differentiated as the child matures. One of the earliest indications of self-awareness may be observed when the youngster (usually about the age of ten months) first recognizes himself in the mirror. Some degree of self-awareness, however, is present in a rudimentary fashion as early as age three months, but tends to become more stable around the age of one year; and from this point on, the child's search for a personal identity magnifies. The child from age one on becomes increasingly more capable of differentiating himself from others. Self-awareness, however, does not suddenly appear in an "all-or-none fashion"; to the contrary, it develops gradually and tends to become more stable with maturity; once the child masters self-awareness, it becomes increasingly apparent and he becomes capable of distinguishing between "I," "you," "mine," and "yours." The child's awareness of his distinctiveness from others emerges before his perception and conception of many of the characteristics that comprise what he calls "himself." An early indication of self-awareness emerges when the child begins actively to control objects in his environment, by grasping and manipulating them. The child, as he attempts to gain mastery over his environment, repeats activities which provide gratification (for example, when the infant constantly drops objects from his highchair; a tendency which Piaget calls secondary or tertiary responses or actions). Another important aspect of a growing sense of self-awareness is illustrated when we observe the child's growing perception, understanding, and acceptance of his own body. Body image is essential in the development of a sense of self. Many writers, unfortunately, have tended to de-emphasize the role that one's perception of his physique plays in determining self-perception.

Because of my conviction that perception of one's physique plays a major role in one's perception of self, I include a number of items in the *Culture-Free Self-Esteem Inventory for Children* which are designed to assess the youngster's perception of his body. This inventory is routinely adminstered to all youngsters who are referred to me for therapy, and it has been observed that approximately 95 percent of these youngsters answer "no" to the item, "I am as good looking as most boys and girls." Self-awareness, furthermore, is affected to some degree when children recognize and attend to sexual differences; that is, when they realize for the first time that boys and girls are somewhat different physically. Youngsters generally are keenly interested in anatomical differences between the sexes, and most accept these differences in stride without difficulty. Some youngsters, however, find this discovery disturbing. Psychoanalytical theorists, for instance, would explain this by arguing that girls feel that they have been "castrated" because they do not possess a penis, and as a consequence they feel inferior and experience "penis envy."

A noteworthy observation is the development of the self is evident when the child begins to assert himself as he interacts with others. For instance, at about the age of two years, most children are extremely negativistic and typically say "no" before they say "yes." This process is a normal one, which represents the beginning stages in a process which will eventually lead to a full sense of autonomy. The toddler, as he strives for autonomy, constantly tests his powers of self-assertion, which is a major step in the development of self-awareness. During this stage the child begins to compete with others and constantly compares himself with peers. Many children are possessive during this stage and almost constantly use the term "mine" in relation to their personal possessions (e.g., objects and parental figure). A vivid illustration of this process is provided by our very young daughter, who makes it quite clear to her playmates that I am "her" daddy by stating quite frankly that "Jim is my daddy." This orientation toward comparison, competition, and assertiveness, is very important in the development of self-perception, because it means that the child is using others as a standard against which to measure himself.

Significant Others and Development of Self

The child's perception of himself is greatly influenced by his relations with significant others. In our North American culture, mothers or mother surrogates play the most significant role in in the life of young children. Mothers, thus, are usually the most powerful determinants of self-perception in their children. She, then, is a major force which determines if her child will view himself positively or negatively.

Support for this position is provided by Sullivan (1947), who states that the self-system has its origins in interpersonal relationships and is influenced profoundly by "reflected appraisals." Sullivan's comments indicate that, if significant others communicate to the child the feeling that he is approved of, respected, and liked, he will develop a sense of self-acceptance and respect for himself and others as well. Conversely, if significant others (e.g., parents, teachers) communicate to the child that he is not worthy and generally tend to belittle him, blame him, and reject him, he will tend to view himself as being unworthy. Further support for this position is provided by Carl Rogers (1951), who states that parents should provide unconditional positive regard for their children rather than conditional positive regard. According to Rogers, parents should communicate to the child that he is loved, accepted, wanted, simply because "he is who he is," and that this prizing, loving, caring-for is not conditional or dependent on the behavior the child emits.

Self-Image

Self-image develops as the individual matures and interacts with significant others. It is different for everyone and represents the person's image of himself as an individual who is somewhat unique from all others." The individual is a product of both physical and psychological properties, so the self-image is representative of both these dimensions, and thus, possesses physical and psychological components. The physical component of self-image possesses both function and structure; every organ that is conceived of as doing a given job is included in the individual's physical self-image. Organs, in addition, are given different values which are determined by the conceived functional value of the particular organ (e.g., the heart is typically more highly valued than the hand, and the hand is usually valued more highly than a finger).

The psychological component of the self-image is similar to the physical component in many aspects. For instance, every character trait plays a major role in the individual's psychological component of self-image, and it possesses a hierarchy of traits which are assigned values that are determined by their conceived functional value to the organism's conceptual thinking process. The conceptual aspect of the individual's self-image is of prime importance, for it sets the stage and determines the behavioral responses of the person. For instance, it has been found that individuals employ compensatory maneuvers and emphasize good aspects of the self-image to compensate for conceived bad or negative portions (e.g., "I may not be pretty, but at least I am honest").

If we are to understand the status of one's self-image, we must assess each person individually. We must not concern ourselves with the person's basic or actual self, but must analyze the individual's conceptual value of the self. We must look at his history of early experiences and interactions with significant others because these are the major determinants of one's self-image. Self-image, thus, is an interpersonal phenomenon which is determined by early experiences with significant others. Self-image then is comprised of those traits that have proved to be useful in evoking a certain desirable response from significant others. Traits that do not have recognized interpersonal value, are not included in self-image. The child, as a consequence of interaction, tends to identify with those significant others who gratify his basic needs and tends to rebel against or respond with acquiescence to those caretakers who do not gratify his needs for security (basic trust).

The first year of life is most important in the development of self-image, and each subsequent year generally becomes of lesser importance, until the image is essentially complete in adolescence. Parents are usually the most significant others and as a consequence have the greatest influence in shaping the lives of young children. Other individuals outside the family (e.g., teachers, ministers, etc.) may become significant others; but their impact tends to be of lesser importance than parents, because of the time at which they generally enter the picture.

The maturing young child tends to accept the standards of others literally, without critical judgment (e.g., "mother knows best") and tends to maintain these standards in spite of opposition from outside sources. For instance, if there are discrepancies or incongruence between cultural values and those of significant others, the youngster generally adopts those of significant others. We therefore have sons who are basically like dad, and the statement "like father, like son" continues to have relevance. If we did not have significant others to provide pressures, values, and attitudes which foster development of self-image and give it content, the maturing child—and later, the adult—would not have anything concrete and reliable to measure up to. He therefore would not have any consistent frame reference or "compass" to assist him in charting his life course; he would experience a considerable degree of self-estrangement; and life would be chaotic, erratic, and extremely turbulent.

Once the self-image has been formed, the individual behaves in accordance with its demands, accepting experiences that are consistent or congruent with it and rejecting, denying, or distorting those that are incongruent with it.

It is important, however, to note before concluding this section, that although the self is fairly stable once maturity occurs, changes in the self—and self-esteem in particular—can occur if proper interventive procedures are instituted (see Chapter 8). Once the self-image has stabilized, some form of intervention is needed in order for it to experience significant changes.

Self/Personality/Ego

A review of psychological literature typically reveals that the concepts of *self*, *personality*, and *ego* are often used interchangeably. Admittedly, it is cumbersome and often difficult to clearly differentiate between the terms; but they nevertheless are distinguishable; and appropriate distinctions must be made if they are to be understood and used appropriately.

We postulate that the self, which is the governing agent and core of the psyche, develops first; and the personality and ego are its sequential derivatives. The workings of the self, its personality, and its ego are closely interrelated and represent one unitary interpenetrating psychological organization.

Self

The self is a total unitary phenomenon which is present at birth and becomes more differentiated as the child matures and interacts with significant others. It is the original psychological apparatus that coordinates activities which include sensing, remembering, perceiving, imagining, thinking, feeling, and emoting. The self, therefore, is a knower and an object of knowledge as well. It is the organizing agent which unifies the somewhat diverse functions of the personality and ego.

Personality

G. W. Allport (1937) lists the following five types of psychological definitions of personality.

1. *Omnibus definitions.* These definitions usually begin with the phrase, "Personality is the sum-total of . . . ." Such a definition expresses an aggregate or collection of properties or qualities. An example is the definition by Morton Prince (1924), that "personality is the sum-total of all the biological innate dispositions, impulses, tendencies, appetites, instincts of the individual, and

the acquired dispositions and tendencies acquired by experience" (p. 532). Allport criticized the omnibus definition because such mere listing of characteristics leaves out the most important aspect of mental life as Allport saw it:

... the presence of orderly arrangement. The mere cataloging of ingredients defines personality no better than the alphabet defines lyric poetry (p. 44).

2. *Integrative and configurational definitions.* These definitions stress the organization of personal attributes, as suggested in H. S. Warren and L. Carmichael's (1930) definition of personality as:

... the entire organization of a human being at any stage of his development (p. 333).

3. *Hierarchial definitions.* This type of definition involves the specification of various levels of organization, usually with an innermost image or self which dominates. An example is the definition of William James (1890) which is expressed in terms of four selves: the material self, the social self, the spiritual self, and a core category, the pure ego or self-of-selves.

4. *Definitions in terms of adjustment.* These definitions have often been preferred by psychologists and biologists whose view of man emphasizes adaptation or survival and evolution, as in E. J. Kempf's (1921) definition, where he states that personality is:

... the integration of those systems of habits that represent an individual's characteristic adjustments to his environment.

5. *Definitions in terms of distinctiveness.* This type of definition is illustrated by Shoen's (1930) statement that:

... personality is the organized system, the functioning whole or unity of habits, dispositions and sentiments that mark off any one member of a group as being different from any other member of the same group (p. 397).

Allport felt that definitions of personality would emphasize the following main properties; they should reflect an organization of properties that refer to general styles of life and modes of adaptation to one's surroundings, and should also reflect the idea of the progressive growth and development of individuality or distinctiveness. His definition reflects this sentiment:

Personality is the dynamic organization within the individual of those psychophysical systems that determine his unique adjustments to his enviroment (p. 48).

A key word in Allport's (1937) definition of personality is *psychophysical*, which indicates that personality is neither exclusively mental, nor exclusively neural (p. 48).

Although Allport's definition is one of the most widely cited ones of personality, he nevertheless saw the need to revise it somewhat and in 1961 defined personality as being:

... the dynamic organization within the individual of those psychophysical systems that determine his characteristic behavior and thought.

The personality is the first and most important derivative of the self to develop. A portion of the self gradually transforms into the personality as a consequence of the self's continuous efforts to become more competent or effective in adjusting to the demands of the external environment. The personality, therefore, represents the self's mode of adjustment to environmental demands (e.g., its unique mode of survival). The personality represents the self's organized mode of adjustment, it is well anchored in the self; and its mode of functioning is determined by the self. The personality, therefore, is not independent of the self and cannot divorce itself from self-scrutiny. It is used by the self as an adaptive mechanism for dealing with the outside world. The type of personality that is derived from the self determines the degree of success the self will subsequently experience in its interactions with the external environment. Success or lack of success in dealing with environmental demands, however, is not dependent on the functioning of psychological mechanisms alone, but is also highly influenced by one's culture. For example, if the self provides a personality that is kind, obliging, honest, hardworking, it would theoretically experience a great deal of success in a democratic society. The same type of personality, however, may not be as successful in a society in which the mode of operation is "everyone for himself" or "get others before they get you."

Ego

The ego is the second derivative of the self to develop, and represents an extension of the personality. It is a derivative of the self and extension of the personality which has autonomy and unique properties of its own. It is an acquired phenomenon which is admittedly quite similar to the personality in constitution, but plays a role that is different from the one played by the personality. The personality, for example, tends to be fairly stable over time and from situation to situation, whereas the ego tends to vary from time to time; and its contents generally change fairly frequently. The ego, as a consequence of this variability, may be occupied for the moment with a given activity and shortly afterwards with a totally different task; thus, the ego is the essential force for meeting specific adjustment demands at a given time, while the personality is the force employed by the self for typical or general forms of adjustment. The ego, for example, would be the central force for dealing with acute crisis, whereas the personality would be the central force in general, day-to-day adjustment.

A schematic presentation of development of the self, personality, and ego is presented in Figure 3.1.

FIGURE 3.1. *A Schematic Presentation of the Self, Personality, and Ego.*

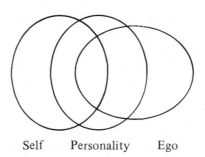

Self   Personality   Ego

Ideal Self

The ideal self refers to the individual's view of that he aspires to be or feels that he "ought to be." Take for example the case of Billy, who is achieving at the 80th percentile. Billy, who feels he is not living up to his aspirations, may be dissatisfied with his achievements, although his teachers and parents are quite pleased with his performance. Most youngsters experience discrepancies between the ideal self and the self as-it-is, or the real or actual self. When the discrepancy between the ideal self and the real or actual self is large, and the actual self occupies the lower level (aspirations greater than accomplishments) the greater is the probability that self-esteem will be negatively affected and the greater the probability of psychopathology. For example, subjects in R. H. Seiden's study (1966) of suicides at the University of California, Berkeley, were all high achievers who were generally earning grades above the median grade point average, but typically felt that they were not earning high enough grades; they tended to perceive themselves negatively, developed depression, and subsequently committed suicide.

The construct of the ideal self which is usually used to describe one's optimal level of personal aspiration, occurs as a result of the child's identification with people whom he loves, admires, or fears. The parents are the first and usually the most important objects of identification. Subsequent important objects of identification include teachers, heroes, movie stars, athletes, etc. The developing child usually identifies with parents initially and then gradually extends his identifications to others. This process of identification enables the child to imitate the values and attitudes of others and is essential in the development of the ideal self, or ego ideal. Figure 3.2 presents the sequence of identifications which determine ideal-self development.

FIGURE 3.2. *Proposed Sequential Development of the Ideal Self.*

Stage	Age	Object of Identification
Childhood	6—8	Parent/Family Member
Middle Childhood/Early Adolescence	8—16	Glamorous/Attractive People
Late Adolescence	16+	Composite of Identifications

The data presented in Figure 3.2 indicates that the youngster initially identifies with parents or family members, expands his identifications to include attractive individuals beyond the family circle, and finally is able to integrate or synthesize all previous identifications into a composite.

R. J. Havighurst, M. Z. Robinson, and M. Dorr (1946), in a study designed to measure the development of the ideal self, asked boys and girls aged eight to eighteen to write a brief essay on the topic, "the person I would like to be like." The participating subjects were requested to:

> . . . describe in a page or less the person you would most like to be when you grow up. This may be a real person, or an imaginary person. He or she may be a combination of several people. Tell something about this person's age, character,

appearance, occupation, and reactions. If he is a real person, say so. You need not give his real name if you do not want to (p. 227).

After analyzing the responses of subjects, Havighurst's research group developed the following categories:

I.=P Parents and other relatives of the parental or grandparental generation.

II.=S Parent-surrogates: teachers, neighbors of the parental generation.

III.=G Glamorous adults: people with romantic or ephemeral fame due to the more superficial qualities of appearance and behavior (e.g., movie stars, military figures, athletes). Note: Characters in comic strips or radio dramas are included here, though they may be imaginary (e.g., Superman, Dick Tracy).

IV.=H Heroes, people with substantial claim to fame, usually tested by time (e.g., Florence Nightingale and Abraham Lincoln). However, certain living persons are placed in this category (e.g., important political or military figures).

V.=A Attractive and successful young adults within the individual's range of observation. These are usually young people who live in the community, or go to a local college or lead a scout group, or are related to the subject's older siblings, cousins, young uncles or aunts. They can be observed by the subject in three dimensions, as it were—going about their daily work, making moral decisions, getting along with family and friends, preparing for an occupation.

VI.=C Composite or imaginary characters: These are abstractions of a number of people. Sometimes they appear to be wholly imaginary; other times they are clearly a coalescence of qualities of two or three real persons.

VII.=M Age mates or youths, only two or three years older than the subject. While the directions sought to prevent the naming of these, some were named.

VIII.=NC Miscellaneous responses, not classifiable among those mentioned above: A fairly frequent response in this category is "myself" (p. 228).

The responses emitted by subjects are presented in Figure 3.3. The data presented in Figure 3.3 indicate that responses fall mainly into four categories, those of parents, glamorous adults, attractive and visible young adults, and composite imaginary characters. Parent-surrogates (e.g., teachers and older adults) are seldom mentioned; and heroes are rarely named.

The number of groups identified in the study and the number of papers submitted by each group is given in Figure 3.4. The data presented in Figure 3.4 indicate that there were nine groups identified in the study, which submitted 608 papers altogether.

1. Ten-, eleven-, and twelve-year-olds in a typical small midwestern community.
2. Sixth-graders (age 11 and 12) in an industrial section of Chicago.
3. Fifth- and sixth-graders (age 11 and 12) in an industrial community.
4. Girls at a Chicago settlement house (age 11 to 14), mostly of Italian extraction.
5. Seventh- and eighth-graders (age 13 to 14) in an industrial community.
6. Middle-class black children (age 12 to 14) in Baltimore.
7. Ninth-graders (age 14 to 15) in a lower-middle-class suburb in Chicago.
8. Boys (age 16 to 17) in a vocational high school in Chicago.
9. Sixteen- and seventeen-year-olds in a typical small midwestern community.

FIGURE 3.3. *Classifications of People Described as "My Ideal Self" (Boys).*

Group		A	B	C	D	E	F	G	H	I
Number of Papers		60	26	89	—	94	85	106	31	48
Category										
I	P	7	23	11	—	16	7	16	3	6
II	S	0	0	0	—	0	2	2	0	11
III	G	12	32	47	—	23	37	40	22	6
IV	H	3	6	11	—	10	5	3	13	2
V	A	53	30	23	—	21	15	24	9	25
VI	C	25	6	8	—	28	28	15	19	48
VII	M	0	0	0	—	2	1	0	13	2
VIII	NC	0	3	0	—	0	5	0	19	0

Source: Havighurst, R. J., Robinson, M. Z., and Dorr, M. 1946. The development of the ideal self. *Journal of Educational Research* 40:241-257. Reprinted by permission of the senior author and Denbar Publications.

FIGURE 3.4. *Classifications of People Described as "My Ideal Self" (Girls).*

Group		A	B	C	D	E	F	G	H	I
Number of Papers		100	36	105	17	114	70	80	—	86
Category										
I	P	6	32	14	6	11	7	20	—	3
II	S	2	0	2	0	4	12	9	—	1
III	G	16	17	27	23	21	37	21	—	1
IV	H	2	3	3	6	1	7	7	—	4
V	A	36	13	25	18	25	18	23	—	28
VI	C	33	22	23	29	35	18	15	—	61
VII	M	3	8	6	12	3	1	5	—	2
VIII	NC	0	5	0	6	0	0	0	—	0

Source: Havighurst, R. J., Robinson, M. Z., and Dorr, M. 1946. The development of the ideal self. *Journal of Educational Research* 40:241-257. Reprinted by permission of the senior author and Denbar Publications.

Havighurst, Robinson, and Dorr (1946) concluded the following from the data collected and analyzed in their study:

1. The ideal self starts to develop in childhood as an identification with a parental figure, moves during the middle childhood and early adolescence as a composite of desirable characteristics which may be symbolized by an attractive, visible, young adult, or may be simply an imaginary figure.
2. Parents or members of the parental generation play a declining role in the ideal self as it is described by children after the age of eight or ten.
3. Glamorous adults play major roles in the child's ego-ideal between the ages of ten and fifteen.
4. Children and adolescents from families of lower socioeconomic status generally lag behind those of middle socioeconomic status in the progression through the stage of selection of a glamorous adult as an ideal (pp. 237-238).

The Nature of Self-Esteem

Psychologists, as a group, generally agree that humans experience a need for self-esteem. What we have not determined are the reasons why we need self-esteem and the conditions we must satisfy if we are to achieve self-esteem. Psychologists, furthermore, realize that there is a relationship between the degree of one's self-esteem and the degree of his mental health. Again, what we have not been able to sort out, are the nature and causes of this relationship. There is also concensus that there is a relationship between the nature and degree of an individual's self-esteem and his motivation (e.g., his behavior in the areas of work, play, love, interpersonal relationships).

Many of the issues just mentioned remain unresolved, but a number of theorists (e.g., N. Branden [1969] in his work entitled *The Psychology of Self-Esteem*), provides noteworthy insights into the nature of self-esteem. For instance, Branden states that self-esteem has two interrelated aspects: It entails a sense of personal efficacy and a sense of personal worth. It is the integrated sum of self-confidence and self-respect. It is the conviction that one is competent to live and is worthy of living (p. 110).

The summary by Branden just presented emphasizes two important phenomena: self-confidence and self-respect. Self-confidence denotes confidence in one's own cognitive processes and refers to the conviction that one is competent to think, to judge, to know. Self-respect refers to a moral appraisal which is based on a statement or value judgment of what is "right or wrong." The need for self-respect is a value judgment; the individual needs self-respect because he cannot divorce himself from values and value judgments. All humans behave in accordance with values, whether they be conscious or subconscious, rational or irrational, self-serving or life-negating. We at all times judge ourselves in accordance with some standard which determines our evaluation of self.

Self-esteem, according to Branden, is the most important value judgment the individual makes. His point of view is summarized as follows:

There is no value judgment more important to man, no factor more decisive in his psychological development and motivation, than the estimate he possesses of himself. This estimate is ordinarily experienced by him, not in the form of a conscious, verbalized judgment, but in terms of a feeling, a feeling that can be hard to isolate and identify because he experiences it constantly; it is part of every other feeling, it is involved in his every emotional response. Man's view of himself is necessarily implicit in all value responses. Any judgment entailing the issue "Is this for me or against me?" entails a view of the "me" involved. His self-evaluation is an omnipotent factor in man's psychology. The nature of his self-evaluation has profound effects on an individual's thinking processes, emotions, desires, values, and goals. It is the single most significant key to his behavior. To understand an individual psychologically, one must understand the nature and degree of his self-esteem and the standards by which he judges himself (pp. 109-110).

Authentic versus Inauthentic Self-Esteem

A major problem that consistently arises in the study of self-esteem is the great difficulty which is usually experienced when one attempts to ascertain valid responses from subjects. For instance, clinicians generally find it extremely difficult to control for faking, either positively or negatively. The problem is even more acute when we are working with children, who generally feel compelled to make statements that they consider to be appropriate or what they feel the examiner expects. Children's responses, consequently, in many instances are not valid indicators of the youngster's current state of affairs. This disposition, to fake, is emphasized by Branden (1969), who states that self-esteem is a fundamental need of man. It is a need that cannot be avoided; and those who fail to achieve self-esteem, or who fail to a significant degree in their search for self-esteem, strive to fake it. Because they fail to ascertain self-esteem, they attempt to hide behind a facade and display psuedo-self-esteem. Psuedo- or inauthentic self-esteem, according to Branden, is an irrational pretense at self-value. It is a non-rational self-protective device designed to reduce anxiety and enhance a sense of security. It (inauthentic self-esteem) is maintained by use of defense mechanisms (e.g., repression, rationalization, denial, projection). Authentic self-esteem, on the other hand, is maintained or enhanced by actions that are in accordance with the individual's moral code. The authentic individual is motivated by reality and emits behaviors that are consistent with his standards. He is confident in himself and is motivated by love of self, whereas the inauthentic individual is defensive and motivated by the fear that he is not worthy. Branden lists the following categories of defenses which he feels inauthentic individuals generally employ.

1. The man who is obsessed with being popular, who feels driven to win the approval of every person he meets, who clings to the image of himself as "likeable," who in effect, regards his appealing personality as his means of survival and the proof of his personal worth.

2. The woman who has no sense of personal identity and who seeks to lose her inner emptiness in the role of a sacrificial martyr for her children, demanding in exchange "only" that her children adore her, that their adoration fill the vacuum of the ego she does not possess.

3. The man who never forms independent judgments about anything, but who seeks to compensate by making himself authoritatively knowledgeable concerning other men's opinions about everything.

4. The man who works at being aggressively "masculine," whose other concerns are entirely subordinated to his role as woman-chaser, and who derives less pleasure from the act of sex than from the act of reporting his adventures to the men in the locker room.

5. The woman whose chief standard of self-appraisal is the "prestige" of her husband, and whose psuedo-self-esteem rises or falls according to the number

of men who court her husband's favor.

6. The man who feels guilt over having inherited a fortune, who has no idea of what to do with it, and proceeds frantically to give it away, clinging to the "ideal" of altruism and to the vision of himself as a humanitarian, keeping his psuedo-self-esteem afloat by the belief that charity is a moral substitute for competence and courage.

7. The man who has always been afraid of life and who tells himself that the reason he is superior is "sensitivity," who chooses his clothes, his furniture, his books, and his bodily posture by the standard of what will make him appear idealistic (p. 151).

Self-Esteem, High and Low

Although it is difficult to determine an individual's true perception of himself by observing his responses on a self-report inventory, research indicates that inventories used in conjunction with other clinical diagnostic measures, are fairly accurate in differentiating individuals who possess low self-esteem from those who possess high self-esteem. A major problem inherent in self-report inventories is that they are generally fairly weak in their ability to account for "faking," either positively or negatively. Some scales however (e.g., Battle (1976, 1981) contain items designed to identify defensive individuals who feel compelled to provide reports of self that are not consistent with the actual state of affairs. The problem, nevertheless, continues to exist and is compounded to a greater degree by the fact that we humans possess such a great need for a positive view of ourselves, that we will evade, repress, or distort our judgment, if it is necessary to do so in order to avoid facing facts that would affect our self-appraisal adversely (i.e., when a man lacks self-esteem, he feels compelled to fake it).

In spite of the inherent difficulties in ascertaining valid perceptions of self-worth, research findings typically indicate that individuals who possess low self-esteem generally tend to differ from individuals who possess high self-esteem. Findings reported by a number of investigators (e.g., Coopersmith 1967) indicate that there are distinguishing features which characterize individuals who possess high or low self-esteem. For instance, A. R. Cohen (1957) states that individuals who possess high self-esteem, as compared to those with low self-esteem, are characterized by tendencies to protect themselves from negative self-evaluation. They are also more effective in their ability to evaluate an objective failure as a small failure and an objective success as a large success.

High Self-Esteem

Coopersmith, in *Antecedents of Self-Esteem* (1967), presents the following general characteristics of individuals who possess high self-esteem.

1. Individuals with high self-esteem tend to be more effective in meeting environmental demands than those with low self-esteem.

2. People with high self-esteem tend to adopt an active and assertive position in meeting environmental demands.

3. High self-esteem is associated with such terms as self-respect, superiority, pride, self-acceptance, and self-love.

4. People with high self-esteem tend to be more independent in conformity-inducing situations, and to manifest greater confidence that they will succeed, than individuals who possess low self-esteem.
5. High self-esteem individuals tend to be popular with their peers.
6. An individual with high self-esteem is apt to attend to others only to the extent that he esteems them.
7. High self-esteem individuals tend to participate in more exploratory and independent activities than do individuals with low self-esteem.
8. High self-esteemed individuals tend to defend themselves well against threats and demeaning attempts by others.
9. High self-esteem individuals tend to possess greater confidence in their ability to deal with events; anxiety is less likely to be aroused in them and they tend to have a greater ability to resist the negative implications of social judgments.
10. High self-esteem individuals tend to be quite capable of defending themselves against threats of their adequacy.

Low Self-Esteem

Cohen (1957), differentiating between individuals who possess low self-esteem and those who esteem themselves highly, states that individuals who esteem themselves lowly, and do not protect themselves from negative evaluation, generally tend to evaluate an objective failure as being a very poor performance and a good success as being a small success.

Coopersmith (1967) states that individuals who possess low self-esteem are characterized by the following:

1. Individuals with low self-esteem tend to withdraw from others and experience consistent feelings of distress.
2. People with low self-esteem tend to be more intropunitive and passive in adapting to environmental demands and pressures than individuals who possess high self-esteem.
3. Low self-esteem tends to be equated with inferiority, timidity, self-hatred, lack of personal acceptance, and submissiveness.
4. People low in self-esteem tend to exhibit higher levels of anxiety and are more likely to exhibit more frequent psychosomatic symptoms and feelings of depression than individuals with high self-esteem.
5. People with low self-esteem tend to be isolates who seldom select one another. These individuals tend to feel that they have greater difficulties forming friendships than do others. There does not appear to be any relationship, however, between self-esteem and group membership. Persons of all levels of confidence and assurance are equally likely to join social groups, but the roles they play are different.
6. Low self-esteem individuals tend not to resist social pressures.
7. Individuals with low self-esteem are more likely to remain quiet, if they feel dissent will evoke personal attack. They are often unwilling to express contrary opinions, even when they know they are correct, and generally tend to react strongly to criticism.
8. Low self-esteem individuals tend to be invisible members of a group; they,

for example, rarely serve as leaders.

9. Low self-esteem individuals tend to lack the confidence to respect the critical appraisal of others, and remain defeated and exposed in their real or imagined deficiencies.

10. Individuals with low self-esteem tend to be self-conscious when talking to others. They tend to be quite conscious of their inadequacies whether they be real or imagined.

11. Low self-esteem individuals, when distracted by personal concerns, will likely turn inward and dwell upon themselves than individuals with high self-esteem.

In addition to Coopersmith's list I believe that the following are additional characteristics of individuals who possess low self-esteem.

1. Low self-esteem individuals tend to be low in initiative and basically non-assertive in their interactions with others.

2. Low self-esteem individuals tend to be more anxious than individuals who possess high self-esteem. These individuals tend to worry and to be pessimistic in their views concerning the future.

3. Low self-esteem individuals tend to be more prone to employing the defenses of projection and repression than individuals who esteem themselves highly.

4. Low self-esteem individuals tend to be more susceptible to developing obsessive-compulsive reactions than persons who esteem themselves highly.

5. Low self-esteem individuals tend to be more timid, shy, and predisposed to withdrawal than individuals who esteem themselves highly.

6. Low self-esteem people tend to be indecisive and usually vacillate when confronted with obstacles.

7. Low self-esteem individuals are more prone to emitting self-defeating responses and developing self-punishing modes of behavior than individuals who esteem themselves highly.

8. Low self-esteem individuals tend to conform more readily to social pressure and exhibit a greater degree of dependence than individuals who esteem themselves highly.

It is obviously easy to differentiate between individuals who possess low self-esteem and those who possess high self-esteem. The problem, however, becomes more acute as the differential between high and low self-regard diminishes. It is more difficult to differentiate separate categories or characteristics for individuals who possess intermediate degrees of self-esteem. The characteristics just listed, nevertheless, have purpose and extend our knowledge of the differentials in self-regard among individuals. The following hypothetical monologues present hypothetical illustrations of individuals possessing high, low, and intermediate degrees of self-esteem.

Such a monologue for a person with positive self-attitude would probably run as follows:

I consider myself a valuable and important person, and am at least as good as other persons of my age and training. I am regarded as someone worthy of respect and consideration by people who are important to me. I'm able to exert an influence upon other people and events, partly because my views are sought and respected, and partly because I'm able and willing to present and defend those views. I have a pretty definite idea of what I think is right, and my judgments are usually borne out by subsequent events. I can control my actions toward the outside world, and have a fairly good understanding of the kind of person I am. I enjoy new and challenging tasks, and don't get upset when things don't go well right off the bat. The work I do is generally of high quality, and I expect to do worthwhile and possibly great work in the future.

A similar monologue by a person with a negative self-attitude would be likely to carry notes of depression and pessimism. This monologue could be expected to proceed along the following general lines:

I don't think I'm a very important or likeable person, and I don't see much reason for anyone else to like me. I can't do many of the things I'd like to do or do them the way I think they should be done. I'm not sure of my ideas and abilities, and there's a good likelihood that other people's ideas and work are better than my own. Other people don't pay much attention to me; and, given what I know and feel about myself, I can't say that I blame them. I don't like new or unusual occurrences, and prefer sticking to known and safe ground. I don't expect much from myself, either now or in the future. Even when I try very hard, the results are often poor, and I've just about given up hope that I'll do anything important or worthwhile. I don't have much control over what happens to me and I expect that things will get worse rather than better.

The self-description of the person with medium self-esteem, in its appraisal and associated experiences, falls between these two monologues. It tends to include a number of positive self-statements, but is more moderate in its appraisals of competence, significance, and expectations. Such a self-description reflects appreciation of the intermediate position of the subject, but is generally favorable in its assessments and conclusions. The person with medium self-esteem regards himself as better than most, but not as good as some select, unusual individuals. In most respects, his opinions are closer to those of people with high self-esteem than to those of people with low self-esteem.

Summary

The self develops early in life as the child matures and interacts with others, and becomes more stabilized and differentiated with age. Parents have the greatest influence on self-development; and, as a consequence, the child's self reflects the appraisals of parents or parent-surrogates. The self-system, thus, has its origins in interpersonal relationships and is influenced profoundly by reflected appraisals (Sullivan 1937). The self is formed early in life as a result of experience with the environment, is built on interpersonal experiences for survival, and becomes a structured and stabilized phenomenon which is highly resistant to change. The self, once established, motivates the individual to choose objectives and goals which are consistent or congruent with it. Experiences that are consistent with the self are perceived accurately, whereas those that are incongruent with the self are generally distorted or denied. The individual perceives in ways that are consistent with his concept of self. Since some perceptions of self may cut across the individual's experience with the environment and because the self needs a high degree of stability, it puts up mechanisms which either deny the experience or modify it symbolically.

Although the constructs self, personality, and ego are frequently used interchangeably, I feel that distinctions should be made between them. I postulate that the self is the core and governing agent of the psyche, whereas the personality and ego are its derivatives.

Considerable research energies have been directed toward investigating the self in general, but few have been concerned with identifying the influence which determines ideal self-development. One of the most comprehensive studies designed to measure ideal self-development was conducted by Havighurst, Robinson, and Dorr (1946), who found that youngsters initially identify with parents or family members, expand their identifications to include attractive individuals beyond the family circle, and finally integrate or synthesize all previous identifications into a composite.

ENHANCING

II

DEVELOPMENT OF THE SELF

4

ANTECEDENTS AND CORRELATES OF THE SELF

Psychologists have reported various antecedents and correlates of self-esteem. To summarize the antecedents and correlates of self-esteem is by no means a simple task. In this chapter we will attempt to summarize some of the most important antecedents and correlates of self-esteem reported in the literature.

A number of theorists, including M. Rosenberg (1965), S. Coopersmith (1967), and me (1977), have found self-esteem to be significantly correlated with: (1) social status, (2) depression, (3) age, (4) sex, and (5) mental health.

Social Status and Self-Esteem

Social status, to the dismay of many, appears to be only weakly related to self-esteem. Support for this position is provided by V. T. Thompson (1972) in his study of the relationship between age and economic advantage. Thompson found that there was no significant difference between the self-esteem of young economically advantaged and disadvantaged children. He did discover, however, a significant difference between the self-esteem of older (high school) advantaged and disadvantaged children, favoring the economically advantaged subjects. His advantaged subjects reported more positive concepts than his economically disadvantaged subjects. Thompson concluded that:

> . . . It is logical to assume that disadvantagement will ultimately affect self-concept and that this effect increases as the disadvantaged person grows older (p. 53).

Stanley Coopersmith (1967) found that the relationship between social class and self-esteem is positive, but weak. Data derived from his study indicates that individuals in the high (upper-middle) social class are more likely to have higher esteem than individuals in the middle-middle and working classes, but that this differential is not significant. Other theorists, however (e.g., Rosenberg 1965), have found self-esteem to be significantly related to social class. Marshall Rosenberg's results, however, appear to be attributable to sample size rather than real differences between the groups employed in the study. For instance, Coopersmith's percentages and Rosenberg's percentages are almost identical, but Rosenberg assessed 1,640 subjects, whereas Coopersmith assessed only 80.

Depression and Self-Esteem

Clinicians generally agree that depression tends to be associated with low self-esteem. For instance, A. T. Beck and A. Beamesderfer (1974) suggest that characteristics of depression include pessimism, sense of failure, self-dislike, social withdrawal, and somatic preoccupation. Coopersmith (1967) states that individuals who possess low self-esteem tend to experience feelings of distress, self-hatred, psychosomatic symptoms, and feelings of depression.

In a study of the relationship between self-esteem and depression (1978), I administered the *Culture-Free Self-Esteem Inventory for Adults* and Beck's *Depression Inventory* to 129 males and females enrolled in an introductory educational psychology course. Findings from the sudy are summarized in Table 4.1.

TABLE 4.1. *Means, Standard Deviations, and Correlations of Two Measures by Sex.*

	Combined Sexes (N = 129)				Males (n = 43)				Females (n = 86)			
	Mean	S.D.	r	p	Mean	S.D.	r	p	Mean	S.D.	r	p
Self-Est.	24.17	5.10	−.55	.01	24.53	4.69	−.53	.01	23.98	5.31	−.56	.01
Depr.	4.57	3.84			4.41	3.48			4.65	4.03		

Note: High self-esteem scores indicate high or positive self-esteem, whereas low depression scores indicate lack of depression.

The data presented in Table 4.1 indicate that self-esteem is significantly related to depression. That is, as self-esteem increases, depression decreases.

One would expect higher correlations than those presented between self-esteem and depression in a clinical population. Thus, a study involving high school students who were referred to me for assessment was conducted. Twenty-six high school students participated in the study. Thirty-four percent of the students were referred for absenteeism; whereas 15 percent were referred because it was felt that they were experiencing depression. The remaining subjects were referred for various reasons—including anxiety, alienation, and apathy. The mean age for participating subjects was 16.0 years. Forty-three percent of the subjects were male; 57 percent were female. The *Culture-Free Self-Esteem*

Inventory for Adults, Form AD, Beck's *Depression Inventory*, and the Depression subscale of the *Mini-Mult* were administered to all participating subjects. Findings of the study are presented in Table 4.2.

TABLE 4.2. *Means, Standard Deviations, and Correlations for All Subjects (N = 26).*

Subscale	Self-Esteem		Depression				MMPI			
	Mean	S.D.	Mean	S.D.	r	p	Mean	S.D.	r	p
Total	16.69	7.46	15.13	12.12	−.75	.01	28.00	6.19	−.75	.01
General	8.03	4.21	15.13	12.12	−.78	.01	28.00	6.19	−.72	.01
Social	5.15	1.82	15.13	12.12	−.34	.05	28.00	6.19	−.42	.01
Personal	3.46	2.73	15.13	12.12	−.61	.01	28.00	6.19	−.73	.01

Note: High self-esteem scores indicate high or positive self-esteem, whereas low depression scores indicate lack of depression.

The high correlations between self-esteem and depression indicate that the two variables are strongly associated in adolescents. Students who earned higher self-esteem scores tended to obtain lower depression scores. These data confirm that depression in adolescents is associated with low self-esteem. Also of notable importance is the observation that the personal facet of self-esteem correlates higher ($r = -.61$ and $-.73$) with depression than the social facet ($r = -.34$ and $-.42$), indicating that depression is a distressful mood characterized by diminished feelings of personal worth. Thus, the personal facet of self-esteem tends to be most closely related to depression. Findings of the study confirm previous empirical observations which indicate that depressed individuals almost always possess low self-esteem.

The following case of a 28 year old male is presented to illustrate the relationship between self-esteem and depression.

Case Report 4.1

Bobby B., 28 years old, married, no children.

Bobby was the only boy in a family of four children. Bobby earned passing marks during the elementary, junior high and senior high years, but his teachers generally commented that they felt he could make better grades. His interactions with peers were fairly typical during the formative years, but the client lacked initiative and perserverance and he rarely assumed leadership roles. After high school Bobby enrolled at a university. After three years the client had studied at three different universities but had accumulated only a few credits. After being dismissed from the third university, Bobby contacted the writer and requested therapy because "he couldn't understand why he continually failed." Intelligence testing revealed that Bobby possessed superior ability. His WAIS Verbal, Performance, and, Full Scaled IQ Scores were 123, 122, and 124 respectively. Personality test results indicated that the client was depressed and possessed very low self-esteem. Analysis of the scores revealed the following:

Subscale	Possible Score	Mean Score	Client's Score	% Rank	t-Score	Classification
Total	32	23.7	11	2	25	Very Low
General	16	12.0	5	2	27	Low
Social	8	6.9	5	30	44	Intermediate
Personal	8	4.9	1	14	37	Very Low

After ten weeks of therapy the client was able to resolve his emotional difficulties and modify his self-defeating patterns. Testing this time indicated that the client was not depressed and that his self-esteem had increased significantly. His self-esteem scores were as follows:

Subscale	Possible Score	Mean Score	Client's Score	% Rank	t-Score	Classification
Total	32	23.7	27	83	60	High
General	16	12.0	13	71	57	High
Social	8	6.9	7	80	60	High
Personal	8	4.9	7	90	63	High

Bobby was able to gain re-admission to the university and on this occasion was able to maintain an average of 80 percent in his classes. He completed his education two years later and is currently successfully employed in an important administrative position.

The empirical data listed above, linking depression to self-esteem, provide quantitative data supporting the position held by many, which states that "depression is significantly associated with low self-esteem." Although this position is generally accepted by psychologists, psychiatrists, and mental health workers in general, heretofore little quantitative data have been presented to confirm this hypothesis. Our data clearly indicate that depression is related to low self-esteem in adults and adolescents. Our findings indicate, moreover, that clinical patients experience lower levels of self-esteem and higher levels of depression than subjects in the general population (See Tables 4.1 and 4.2).

Age and Self-Esteem

Researchers generally agree that self-esteem tends to increase and become more differentiated with age (Grant 1966; Thompson 1972). This position is supported by data I have also reported (1976, 1977), having found that junior high school students scored higher on the *Culture-Free Self-Esteem Inventory for Children* than elementary school pupils. Findings of this study are presented in Table 4.3.

TABLE 4.3. *Means, Standard Deviations, and Correlations by Grade and Sex.*

Grade	Combined Sexes			Males			Females		
	N	Mean	S.D.	n	Mean	S.D.	n	Mean	S.D.
Elem.	198	35.23	7.46	115	34.87	7.88	83	36.11	6.51
Jr. High	117	37.20	6.66	53	37.56	6.85	64	36.72	6.13

Findings presented in Table 4.3 indicate that self-esteem tends to rise with age. Youngsters apparently become more competent in dealing with environmental demands with maturity, and as a consequence tend to evaluate their self-worth more positively.

A thorough review of the literature which deals with the effects of maturity (age) on self-esteem is provided by Ruth Wylie (1961) in her classic work *The Self-Concept*, in which she summarizes the following studies which describes the development of the self-concept:

> Ames's report on nursery school children presents a summary of data in regard to the growing sense of self such as can be derived from verbalizations of self or to others. . . data are objective in that they consist of actual statements and behaviors of (approximately 100-150) subjects. They are, however, selective. Behaviors and verbalizations considered most pertinent data were further selected (Ames 1952, p. 194).

> From these observations we have built up a developmental picture of the sense of self as it appears to change from age to age [from one month through 3½ years] (p. 229).

Additional support for the position that self-esteem tends to rise and become more differentiated with age is provided by H. V. Perkins (1958), who found a significant increase in ideal-self congruence of fourth- and sixth-grade children over a six-month period. He also found that the sixth-grade chidren possessed greater self-ideal congruence than the fourth-grade subjects.

R. J. Havighurst, M. Z. Robinson, and M. Dorr (1946), in their study of the ideal self, observed youngsters over a wide age range (see pp. 52-57). These investigators compared the compositions of youngsters who were asked to describe "the person I would like to be like." Responses fell mainly into four categories: (1) parents or family members, (2) glamorous persons, (3) attractive visible adults, and (4) composite imaginary persons. These investigators found that children's choices tended to move away from the family circle with age. From ages six to eight, parents or some other family member were typical choices; from ages eight to sixteen, children tended to describe glamorous persons, then attractive visible adults, and finally composite imaginary persons.

Although most psychologists assume that the self-concept develops gradually over a period of time, some (e.g., Engel 1959) suggest that it develops earlier than we are generally led to believe. Support for this position is provided by data derived from his study (1959), in which he analyzed test-retest self-concept scores of 172 subjects over a two-year period. Engel identified two groups of boys and girls, tested one group in grades eight and ten, and the other group in grades ten and twelve. Engel found that the average self-self correlation for 23 subjects over a ten-day period was .68, and that the average correlations for the same subjects over a two-year period was .53. The fact that there was no significant difference between the older and younger groups with respect to self-self correlations over the two-year period confirmed Engel's hypothesis, which was based on the assumption that "crystalization of the self-concept is achieved earlier in development" (Wylie 1961, pp. 119-120).

Sex and Self-Esteem

Psychologists and educators generally agree that males and females are conditioned differently from each other in North American society. As a consequence, girls and boys usually choose different roles, and possess somewhat different aspirations and goals. Because of this phenomenon of "social determinism," as some would-be theorists would put it, it is appropriate—and indeed, wise—to assume that boys and girls, males and females, would differ somewhat in phenomenal self-regard. This proposition has been supported by a number of investigators. For instance, Kagan and Moss (1961) found that boys generally perceived themselves as being stronger, larger, more dangerous, darker, and more angular than girls.

In my own research (Battle 1976), I did not discover significant differences in the various dimensions of self-esteem (general, social, school, home) for boys and girls, but noted that boys tend to earn higher self-esteem scores with maturity. For instance, the mean score for elementary-grade girls were found to be somewhat higher than the mean score for elementary-grade boys (boys = 34.87; girls = 36.11); but boys scored higher than girls at the junior high level (boys = 37.61; girls = 36.72).

This trend for males and females continues into the college years. For example, I found the mean self-esteem scores for males and females enrolled in an introductory educational psychology course at the University of Alberta to be 24.12 and 23.45 respectively (1977).

To review adequately the issue of sex-linked self-esteem, we must look closely at the matter of sex stereotypes and cultural expectations of the two genders. We must ask questions such as: What does society expect of males? What does society expect of females? Do society's expectations for males and females differ? What stereotypes do we hold for males and females repectively? Some answers to these questions may be derived from the findings of research by J. P. McKee and A. C. Sheriffs (1957), T. R. Sorbin and B. G. Rosenberg (1955), Sr. M. Amatora (1957), A. R. Kohn and F. E. Fielder (1961), and Piers and Harris (1969).

Mckee and Sheriffs (1957), employing a general rating scale in their studies of male and female stereotypes, found that both male and female college students felt that males were superior to females. The same investigators, using empirical means for determining sex stereotypes, found that the "real selves" of females were more sex-typed than the "real selves" of men, in spite of the fact that the female stereotype was less desirable than the male stereotype.

Sorbin and Rosenberg (1955), employing a modified version of Gough's *Adjective Checklist*, reported that males exceeded females in checking adjectives such as resourceful, mature, logical, adventurous, realistic, deliberate, efficient; whereas females exceeded males in checking adjectives such as feminine, emotional, affectionate, pleasant, and temperamental. Similar results are provided by Zahran (1967) in his study of adolescent males and females. Zahran found significant differences on the various dimensions of self between boys and girls. Girls scored higher on traits such as sociability, dependence, sensitivity, and tolerance; whereas boys were found to be more confident, self-accepting, dominant, and realistic.

Although most researchers report more positive self-evaluations for boys, some investigators (e.g., Amatora 1957; Perkins 1958; Kohn and Fielder 1961) reported higher self-esteem for females; and others (e.g., Piers and Harris 1969) have reported no significant sex differences between the sexes in self-esteem. The area of self-esteem and sex, therefore, remains somewhat unclear. It appears, nevertheless, that society, by way of its conditioning process, shapes the behavior of boys and girls somewhat differently, which subsequently causes boys and girls to perceive themselves somewhat differently.

Mental Health and Self-Esteem

It is difficult for a number of reasons to define the concepts of mental health, adjustment, normalcy, abnormality, etc. A major problem in defining concepts of this nature is that of delineating the criteria for determining: What is mental health? What represents pathology? What is indicative of good or bad adjustment? A number of theorists, nevertheless, have attempted to define mental health. W. A. Scott (1958), for example, in his review of research definitions of mental illness, offers the following:

> Though adjustment appears a more conceptually adequate criterion of mental health than does exposure to treatment, the necessity for considering different personal frames of reference and the demands of different social structures poses seemingly insurmountable obstacles for the establishment of mutually consistent operational definitions. All such difficulties which be "hidden," as it were, under the psychiatric treatment criterion, come to the fore to plague the researcher trying to establish a criterion for adjustment which applies to the treated and nontreated alike (p. 32).

Psychologists, inspite of the difficulties inherent in defining adjustment (either conceptually or operationally), generally agree that low self-esteem is associated with, and in fact may be the cause of, maladjustment. If one accepts this position, it seems logical, therefore, to hypothesize that if "low self-esteem is indicative of maladjustment, then high self-esteem is associated with mental health or adjustment." Support for this thesis is provided by my own work (1978), which demonstrates a strong relationship between self-esteem and depression among college students (p. 75ff). I also found that low self-esteem was associated with adjustment difficulties and learning problems. Additional support for this proposition is provided by M. Rosenberg (1965), who found that individuals with low self-esteem possessed more adjustment problems. My findings reported (1978, 1975) and Rosenberg's (1965), indicate that individuals low in self-esteem would probably tend to be anxious and distressed and as a consequence would probably manifest more psychosomatic symptoms and personal difficulties. This hypothesis was tested by Coopersmith (1967) in his study of the relationship between psychopathology and self-esteem, in which he focused specifically on: (1) general mental health, (2) incidence of psychosomatic symptoms, and (3) acts of destruction. Emotional status of Coopersmith's boys was derived from data received from interviews with children's mothers. Findings derived from the mothers' appraisals of their children's mental health are presented in Table 4.4.

Data presented in Table 4.4 indicate that 60 percent of the low self-esteem group manifested frequent or serious problems, as compared to only 12.5 percent of the high self-esteem group who manifested symptoms of this magnitude. Findings, therefore, reveal a strong, significant, positive relationship between mental health and self-esteem as determined by mothers' reports. That is, mothers felt that their high self-esteem sons possessed fewer and less frequent problems than boys with medium and low self-esteem.

The concept of anxiety (which is associated with low self-esteem) is important to our discussion of mental health and self-esteem. Research findings indicate that there are three general types of responses to anxiety: internalization, withdrawal, externalization. Findings heretofore presented indicate that individuals possessing low self-esteem tend to internalize more frequently psychophysiologic symptoms and generally experience greater subjective distress. Some theorists (e.g., Aichorn 1935) go one step further and assume that externalization as well (e.g., aggressive and antisocial behavior) is a consequence of low self-esteem. Coopersmith (1967) tested Aichorn's hypothesis in his study of the relationship between self-esteem and destructiveness. The findings from his study are presented in Table 4.5.

Findings presented in Table 4.5 reveal a negative relationship between self-esteem and destructiveness. Results indicate that youngsters high in self-esteem tend to be less destructive than those who possess medium and low self-esteem. Children possessing low self-esteem, although more withdrawn and less assertive, apparently are quite capable of venting destructive behavior when it does not involve direct confrontation with others. Their hostility, therefore, is usually directed toward inanimate objects, such as toys, furniture, clothing, etc.

Summary

Although numerous and diverse antecedents and correlates of self-esteem have been reported by investigators, the most comprehensive and meaningful lists of antecedents and correlates has been compiled by Coopersmith. For instance, Coopersmith (1967) found self-esteem to be significantly related to anxiety, mental health, and destructiveness. Other theorists, myself included (1975, 1978), have found self-esteem to be significantly related to depression, adjustment difficulties, and learning problems. Findings of Rosenberg's study (1965) indicate that self-esteem is positively related to social class.

The most powerful and important antecedent of self-esteem is the early parent/child relationship, which determines to a significant degree how the child will subsequently evaluate his worth as an individual. Coopersmith (1967) states that the following are optimal conditions for facilitating positive self-evaluations in children:

1. Almost total acceptance of the child by parents.
2. The establishment of clearly defined and enforced limits for the child.
3. The respect and latitude for individual action that exists within these clearly defined limits.

Coopersmith proposed that, if the above-mentioned conditions are met, the child will develop positive perceptions of self-worth, a condition associated with many important aspects of human functioning, including mental health and academic achievement. The former was discussed in this chapter; the latter will be discussed in detail in Chapter 5.

TABLE 4.4. *Mothers' Appraisals of Their Children's Mental Health.*

	Subjective Self-Esteem					
Mothers' Appraisal	Low		Medium		High	
Marked, Frequent Problems	60.0%	(18)	35.3%	(6)	12.5%	(4)
Limited, Infrequent Problems	40.0%	(12)	64.7%	(11)	85.5%	(28)
Totals	100.0%	(30)	100.0%	(17)	100.0%	(32)

$$x^2 = 15.27 \qquad df = 2 \qquad p = .001$$

Source: Coopersmith, S. 1967. *Antecedents of self-esteem.* San Francisco: Freeman. Reproduced by permission of the publisher and Dr. Coopersmith.

TABLE 4.5. *Destructiveness of Children's Behavior.*

	Subjective Self-Esteem					
Degree of Destructiveness	Low		Medium		High	
Relatively Destructive	60.0%	(18)	35.3%	(6)	12.1%	(4)
Relatively Indestructive	40.0%	(12)	64.7%	(11)	87.9%	(29)
Totals	100.0%	(30)	100.0%	(17)	100.0%	(33)

$$x^2 = 15.84 \qquad df = 2 \qquad p = .001$$

Source: Coopersmith, S. 1967. *Antecedents of self-esteem.* San Francisco: Freeman. Reproduced by permission of the publisher and Dr. Coopersmith.

ENHANCING

III

SELF-ESTEEM AND ACHIEVEMENT

ENHANCING

5

ACADEMIC ACHIEVEMENT AND SELF-ESTEEM

Most people generally agree that self-esteem and achievement are significantly correlated. Research support for this position is provided by G. B. Gillman (1969), who states that the development of a positive self-concept is a necessary prerequisite to academic achievement and should be a major objective of every school that is concerned with the development of productive citizens.

C. Lipton (1963), offers the following remarks concerning the relationship between self-esteem and achievement.

> The roots of desire to learn are deep and multibranched. The development of a self-worth and self-value is one of the most important and significant of these branches. To know oneself and to value oneself contributes mightily to the development of an able learner, a curious learner, and a mature learner (p. 211).

Educators have recognized the importance of self-esteem in the process of achievement for many years and believe strongly that a negative self-concept is a significant factor contributing to low academic achievement.

Advances in attempts to understand the role that self-esteem plays in the achievement process have been limited greatly because there have been few instruments available that reliably assess self-esteem. This problem is vividly illustrated by Ruth Wylie (1961), who concludes that researchers who study the phenomenon of self-esteem generally employ instruments that are questionable. Reliability estimates of the instruments being used, moreover, are rarely provided; and when reliability estimates are presented, they are usually of the split-half or interjudge variety, and rarely provide an indication of test-retest reliability. In an attempt to remedy the problem, I developed a series of self-esteem inventories that I call the *Culture-Free Self-Esteem Inventories for Children and Adults*, which possess acceptable reliability and validity estimates. Psychologists, educators and researchers have found the scales to be valid and reliable measures of self-esteem. The instruments are also effective measures of change due to interventive procedures.

Because of our lack of understanding of the role that self-esteem plays in the learning process, educational programs for children and youth have generally been inadequate. Although educators realize that self-esteem is an important variable effecting achievement, they have typically failed to implement procedures which will enhance self-esteem and, in turn, facilitate achievement. Because of this failure to promote self-enhancement, educational programs have been inadequate in developing youngsters' potential. As a consequence, we have the underachiever, who has grown so rapidly among our youth, that he is close to outnumbering our so-called achievers. The problem of underachievement is a major one in practically all North American school systems: a problem, from my point of view, that is highly associated with low self-esteem.

Underachievement Defined

There are many ways of defining underachievement, but most investigators choose to employ a discrepancy definition. That is, they tend to define underachievement as being representative of a discrepancy between potentiality and actual accomplishments. J. W. Gardner (1961) suggests that underachievement refers to those individuals who demonstrate well above average on intellectual or academic tests, but who fail to develop their potential. In my own study of self-esteem and achievement (1972), I defined an underachiever as being a subject whose *t*-score of his aggregate achievement (report card) was five points or more below his *t*-score derived from his prorated IQ score on the *Canadian Lorge-Thorndike Intelligence Test*.

Definitions of underachievment, at conceptual and operational levels, are important in the study of underachievement. For example, if I had chosen to use a discrepancy score of 15 points or more between aggregate achievement and standardized IQ scores, I would have identified fewer underachievers. Definitions of underachievement, therefore, are important in determining the number and percentage of youngsters we call underachievers.

Percentage of Underachievers

Investigators present different estimates of the number of underachievers, but generally agree that the percentage is high. For example, H. M. Alter (1952) in a study of 1,162 students living in high socioeconomic areas, found a total of 74 (7 percent) of a suburban junior-senior high school population to possess IQ scores of 130 or above on the *California Test of Mental Maturity* (CTMM). He selected 45 of this group of 74 to study and found that 19 (42 percent) were severe underachievers.

Other theorists (e.g., Wedemeyer 1953; Ritter and Thorn 1954; Coleman 1965; and Wolpe 1954) state that between 20 and 50 percent of students work below their potential and as a consequence may be classified as underachievers.

A review of research literature reveals that between 5 and 50 percent of students may be classified as underachievers. These figures however, should not be taken literally, because figures illustrating the degree of underachievement tend to vary from study to study, and are determined to a large extent by the particular method or technique employed to identify underachievers. Results, nevertheless, indicate that the problem is a profound one and that there is a critical need to implement procedures that will assist our young people in developing their potential more effectively.

Sex and Underachievement

A review of studies designed to explore the area of underachievement indicates that males make up the major portion of underachievers among elementary, junior, and senior high school students. A. Davids (1968) states that the underachiever is more likely to be a boy than a girl, and usually possesses poorer work habits and study skills than does his achieving counterpart. He is also likely to be somewhat impulsive, to lack independence and initiative with respect to school work, to have more negative attitudes toward himself and others, and is more likely than his achieving counterpart to resist assuming responsibility for his own behavior.

Although boys generally possess greater unconscious needs for achievement than do girls, they receive lower grades, constitute a higher percentage of discipline cases, and drop out of school earlier. Girls, on the other hand, out-perform boys, but generally give lower estimates of their own intellectual and academic potential than boys. Boys' estimates of their potential tend to be overoptimistic; whereas girls' estimates are somewhat lower initially and become more pessimistic as their educational careers continue (Battle 1976; Fisher and Waetjen 1966; Ford 1967; and Flanagan 1964).

Male underachievers also tend to display more hostility than girls. M. C. Shaw, K. Edison and H. M. Bell (1960), and Shaw and J. Cnubb (1958), employing the Sorbin *Adjective Checklist* as a measure of self-concept, while studying underachieving male and female high school students, found that male underachievers were more hostile and possessed more negative attitudes about themselves.

Chronic underachievement in boys usually commences earlier (grades two and three) than girls (grades six and seven), and male underachievers out number female underachievers two to one. Findings of J. C. Flanagan (1964) and T. R. Ford (1967) indicate that approximately half of all males who are above average in ability are underachievers, whereas only 25 percent of above average females are considered to be underachievers.

Boys are also more apt than girls to be diagnosed as being mentally retarded, placed in special class, remedial programs and classes for the learning disabled. The syndrome of the learning disabled which has attracted considerable attention recently is defined by the United States Office of Education in three clauses: A clause of exclusion, one of discrepancy, and one of denoting malfunctioning.

Clause one. Exclusion. Learning-disabled children are *not* felt to be:

1. Mentally retarded
2. Sensorially deprived
3. Culturally disadvantaged
4. Physically handicapped
5. Primarily emotionally disturbed

Clause two. Discrepancy. Learning-disabled children experience a significant discrepancy between achievement (performance) and potential (ability). The categories under this clause are broad and include all learning disability dimensions, including the following:

1. Auditory receptive language
2. Oral expressive language
3. Reading
4. Written language
5. Mathematics
6. Nonverbal (e.g., gestures, facial expressions)
7. Behavior

Clause three. Malfunctioning.   The learning-disabled youngster is also felt to experience disturbances in the central processes which result in the disruption of:

1. Perception
2. Memory
3. Association
4. Conceptualization

The foregoing definition implies that learning-disabled children possess average to above average ability, but for some reasons are underachieving academically. William Cruickshank (1977) disagrees with the first statement in clause one. He insists that learning disabilities which are a consequence of perceptual processing deficiencies may occur in children of any intellectual level. He argues that learning disabilities are *not primarily* problems due to mental retardation or sensory defects, but insists that learning disabilities have no respect for intellectual level. Learning disabilities, according to Cruickshank, can be experienced by youngsters with IQ below 80 as well as those at any intellectual level. Cruickshank states that the concept of "learning disability" must be defined in terms of its psychoeducational reality. He agrees with N. Hobbs (1975), who states that the syndrome of "learning disability" refers to:

> . . . those children of any age who demonstrate a substantial deficiency in a particular aspect of academic achievement because of perceptual or perceptual-motor handicaps, regardless of etiology or other contributing factors. The term *perceptual* as is used here relates to those mental (neurological) processes through which the child acquired his basic alphabets of sounds and forms. The term *perceptual handicap* refers to inadequate ability in such areas as the following: recognizing fine differences between auditory and visual discriminating features underlying the sounds used in speech and the orthographic forms used in reading; retaining and recalling those discriminated sounds and forms sequentially, both in short- and long-term memory; ordering the sounds and forms sequentially both in sensory and motor-acts . . . ; distinguishing figure-ground relationships . . . ; recognizing spatial and temporal orientations; obtaining closure . . . ; integrating intersensory information . . . ; relating what is perceived to specific motor functions (p. 306).

This definition indicates that learning disabilities would be conceptualized more accurately if we define them as being perceptual processing deficiencies which result in specific learning problems involving one or more or all sensory modalities. The reason for greater learning disabilities and underachievement in boys is unknown. The exact number and percentage of children experiencing learning disabilities is unknown as well. Some authorities state that only one percent of the elementary school population experiences learning disabilities. Others suggest that as high as 50 percent are disabled learners. Lay groups usually offer the figure of 20 percent. The concensus of the majority of the psychologists who have investigated the area of learning disabilities is that between 10 and

ENHANCING

15 percent of school-age youngsters possess some form of learning disability which seriously impairs academic performance. We are certain, however, about the percentage of boys and girls who are diagnosed as being disabled learners. Four times more boys than girls are diagnosed as being disabled learners. One may ask the question, why do more boys experience greater difficulties in learning than girls? That is, why do girls as a group perform so much better than boys? Are there real physical, psychological, emotional differences between the sexes? One reason that girls do better than boys in the early years is due to the fact that most elementary school teachers are females. How many male kindergarten or first-grade teachers do we have? Rarely do we see more than two or three male teachers on the staff of an elementary school. The mere lack of exposure to male stimulus objects to identify with, tends to impede male performance. In response to the second question listed above, there appears to be some physical differences between boys and girls from the onset. For example, H. Bee (1975) states that boys and girls from birth differ in the following ways:

1. Girls are more advanced, as much as four weeks, at birth in the development of bone ossification (hardening) and muscle development, and they remain advanced in these dimensions throughout the early years. This difference is often referred to as a "faster maturational timetable" for girls.
2. Girls begin their adolescent growth spurt sooner and stop sooner, which may be yet another example of the faster maturational process in girls.
3. Girls' physical growth is steadier and more predictable than that of boys. You can get a better estimate of final height from looking at the height of a young girl than you can from a boy.
4. Girls and boys do not differ markedly in physical strength endurance until adolescence; after about ages 12 to 14, boys experience a sharp increase in strength as a result of major changes in musculature; whereas a girl's physical strength remains the same. Put another way, a ten-year-old boy has only about half as much strength as an adult man.
5. At about the same time as boys are developing extra muscle tissue during adolescence, they are also developing a larger heart and lungs, relative to their size, and a greater capacity for carrying oxygen in the blood (i.e., they develop a greater density of red blood cells, in which oxygen is carried). None of these events occur in the growth of girls.
6. Girls from birth onward have a thicker layer of fat directly below the skin than do boys. It gives girls their "softer" appearance; the bones don't show through as much. It also gives girls and women greater tolerance for extremes in temperature; women can withstand extreme cold, for example, much longer than can men because of this extra layer of insulation (p. 101).

There are obviously some differences between boys and girls as indicated here. These differences, however, cannot account for the major portion of variance as far as academic achievement is concerned between the sexes. We must direct our attention to the cultural conditioning process for answers. From birth, girls in our society are conditioned to perform more adequately in the educational setting than boys. They are taught to attend to relevant stimuli, to respond in socially appropriate ways, and to acquire rewards by being good, nice, competent. Boys, on the other hand, are conditioned in ways that are not conductive for success in our formal educational programs. They are conditioned to be aggressive, good athletes, assertive, gregarious—characteristics which do not necessarily foster achievement and learning in our schools.

Characteristics of Underachievers

Most investigators who have studied underachievement have employed comparative studies (i.e., underachievers have been compared to achieving and overachieving peers). An abundant amount of research has been generated in this area; and, as a consequence, lists of characteristics which are specific to underachievers have been recorded in the literature.

J. S. Bruner and A. J. Caron (1959) developed, through empirical analysis, a dynamic and cognitive picture of academic overachievement and underachievement of 64 sixth-grade pupils living in a middle-class community. The investigators administered the *Wechsler Intelligence Scale for Children* to each subject, converted school grades into standard scores, and computed the discrepancy between the two scores. The seven subjects with the greatest discrepancy between IQ score and school achievement score, and whose school performance exceeded IQ score level, were designated as overachievers. The seven subjects who had the greatest discrepancy between IQ and school score, and whose school performance was below IQ level, were designated as underachievers. These investigators, subsequently administered several measures to subjects, which included McCelland's *Thematic Apperception Test*, Sarason's *Anxiety Test*, and some memory procedures which were intended to measure the efficiency of retention for achievement-related material in contrast to neutral materials. Findings from the study indicate that:

1. Overachieving subjects had a higher TAT need-achievement score than underachieving subjects.
2. Overachievers tended to to recall achievement-related words sooner, had less memory interference for achievement related words, and expended more effort to solve problems in competitive situations than underachievers.

E. Burgess (1956), in his study of underachievers, found them to be less adaptive intellectually than their achieving counterparts. Underachievers also tended to overgeneralize, overextend the self, and were lacking in intellectual control and in repression of emotional reactivity. Underachievers were as capable as achievers in establishing rapport in social situations, but were more dependent in their attitudes toward others. Their motivation for academic achievement was weak and they tended to over react to environmental stimulation.

Ralph (1966) found his underachieving group to be less able or willing to compete for high grades. They were less active in school governing affairs and less dependent on the socialization function of the school. Underachievers generally felt that school authority and power was vested in adults, rather than students, but turned to peers rather than teachers and counselors for guidance. They also possessed more negative attitudes toward school and received poorer ratings from teachers.

Data acquired from the literature indicate that underachievers experience more adjustment difficulties than achievers. For instance, C. W. Bresee (1957) compared 44 achievers and 33 high school underachievers on a variety of personality measures. All subjects participating in the study had IQs that were greater than one standard deviation above the mean. Subjects whose grades averaged B+ or better were designated achievers; those whose grades averaged D or worse were designated underachievers. Findings indicate that underachievers possessed more hostility toward self and were more extra-punitive than achievers. Achievers aimed toward more remote goals requiring higher levels of training and also identified more closely with friends, family, and community, and rated higher on altruism.

A number of investigators have reported that underachievers tend to be more socially oriented than overachievers (Blackham 1955; Bishton 1957; Kirsch 1968; Merrill and Murphy 1959). Ralph (1966) states that underachievers tend to be socially oriented to such an extent that this interest takes precedence over academic pursuits. Underachievers tend to be more extrovertive, whereas overachievers are more introverted and generally tend to function more comfortably in the scholastic realm than in the social area. Additional support for the above observations are provided by J. K. Holland (1959) in his study of usefulness. Holland analyzed the scores earned by students of 291 colleges and universities on the *California Psychological Inventory* and the *Scholastic Aptitude Test*. Findings indicate that high achievers were unsociable, lacked poise and self-confidence, were self-depreciating and inflexible, and tended to minimize worries and complaints. The high achievers, however, were conscientious and responsible. Findings from Holland's study indicate that low achievers tend to be poised and socially skillful, flexible, admitted worries and complaints, were impulsive, and possessed less motivation for academic achievement.

G. Gerhart (1958), in his study of over and underachievement of college students, found that overachievers showed greater drive to complete tasks (achievement) and to organize (plan); whereas underachievers showed greater need for variety (change) and higher social motivation (affiliation).

Contributing Factors of Underachievement

There are apparently numerous factors which may impede achievement and contribute to underachievement. Four major variables which may contribute to the process of underachievement are early experiences, socioeconomic environment, parents, and peers.

Early Experiences

Achievement-motivated behavior develops early in childhood; and many theorists—including Birhler, Eriksen, Freud, and Piaget—support the proposition that early experiences have a tremendous impact on later development. Early experiences, therefore, may inhibit or facilitate achievement during later years. The most impressive type of achievement behavior during the first three years of life is expressed in the persistence in sensory-motor activities involving objects. Behavior at this point of development is very concrete and specific to the stimulus-object. Behavior becomes increasingly more cognitive, complex, and abstract as the youngster develops. H. Larsen and collaborators (1962, 1965) state that concentration and persistence in the pursuit of achievement goals increase with age, clearly from four and a half on; failures are tolerated better and more frequent attempts are made to overcome them.

J. Chance (1961), in his study of independence training, found that this form of training was related to later achievement in school. He found that first-grade children whose mothers favored earlier demands for independence made poorer school progress relative to their intellectual level than did children whose mothers favored later independence demands. The difference in levels of achievement was greater for girls than boys and greater in reading than in arithmetic. Chance concluded that earlier independence training may in actuality be a form of greater pressure upon the child as well as a need for the mother to maintain a greater interpersonal relationship between herself and the child.

Psychologists generally agree that early experiences affect achievement motivation, and that this motivation tends to increase with age. Self-esteem, similarly, commences development early in life and becomes more stable as the child matures. The youngster, therefore, brings with him a fairly stable self-concept and achievement pattern when he enters school.

Socioeconomic Environment

Most investigators have reported that underachievers generally come from lower socioeconomic, culturally deprived homes that are characterized by low income, poor housing, large number of children, and working mothers. High achievers, on the other hand, generally come from upper and middle socioeconomic environments. Family size is also associated with socioeconomic classes or groups, and tends to affect achievement. For example, B. C. Rosen and R. Dandrade (1961) found that the influence of family size on the achievement motivation of boys varies with social class, and that upper class, medium-size families produce boys with the highest achievement motivation. Achievement motivation in the middle class tends to be greater in smaller families. Achievement motivation, therefore, generally tends to increase as family size decreases.

Some research findings support the view that the school environment itself may contribute to achievement. For instance, A. B. Wilson (1959) concludes that the particular school environment may be a significant force in steering the motivation of high ability students. His findings indicate that there are differences in achievement and aspiration of gifted high school students that are related to the social-class makeup of the school. Results from his study reveal that students with comparable IQ and similar family backgrounds performed quite differently in schools which were predominantly middle class than they did in schools that were predominantly lower class. In the lower-class school climate, the bright youngster from a typical middle class family tended to achieve less adequately and generally tended to possess a lower level of educational aspiration than did comparably able students in predominantly middle-class schools.

The consensus of psychologists who have explored the relationship between socioeconomic class and achievement, is that higher socioeconomic environments tend to enhance achievement, whereas lower socioeconomic environments tend to promote under-achievement.

Parents

The most powerful influence in the preschool and preadolescent child's life is the parent—a crucial force which can facilitate or impede achievement in children. This parent-child relationship is the most essential one in the development of achievement patterns and self-esteem. Research concerned with the effects of parental dominance at home and achievement at school has resulted in two divergent points of view. On the one hand, authoritorianism has been seen as fostering submissiveness and/or conformity to parents' and teachers' achievement values, to such an extent that school achievement is enhanced. On the other hand, undue pressure and demands on the young child to achieve and exert power through intellectual pursuits are thought to have adverse effects, contributing to rebellion, repressed hostility, and reduced achievement drive.

W. R. Morrow and R. C. Wilson (1961) in their comparative study of 48 bright, high-achieving boys and 48 bright, low-achieving boys, equated in accordance with grade, socioeconomic status, and intelligence, found that parental dispositions differed significantly between the groups. Parents of high-achieving students engaged in more sharing of ideas, activities, and confidences; they were more affectionate, more trusting, more approving, and more encouraging with respect to achievement. A. T. Jersild (1960) stated that self-discovery is a continuous process which affects achievement, and that significant others, especially parents, play the major role in the development of perceptions of self. His position is presented in the following comments:

> Among the earliest experiences which influence the development of the child's view of himself are those with other people . . . . If a child is accepted, approved, respected, and liked for what he is, he will be helped to acquire an attitude of self-acceptance and respect for himself. But if the significant people in his life—at first his parents and later his teachers, peers, and other persons who wield an influence—belittle him, blame him and reject him, the growing child's attitudes toward himself are likely to become unfavorable. As he is judged by others, he will tend to judge himself (p. 123).

The role that parents play in the development of children's perceptions of self was identified by D. Snygg and A. W. Combs (1959), and is reflected in the following passage taken from their book entitled *Individual Behavior*:

> Out of the interaction of the child with the world about him, the individual comes to differentiate more and more clearly his phenomenal self. Obviously, this concept can be only a function of the way he is treated by those who surround him. As he is loved or respected praised or punished, fails or is able to compete, he becomes gradually to regard himself as important or unimportant, adequate or inadequate . . . . The child can see himself only in terms of his experiences and in terms of the treatment he receives from those responsible for his development. Since the phenomenal self is the result of experience, his behavior can be only an outgrowth of the meaning of that experience, and he must necessarily become in truth what he has been labeled by the community which surrounds him (p. 83).

The writings of Jersild (1960) and Snygg and Combs (1959) provide support for the position held by Morrow and Wilson (1961), which holds that democratic parent-child relations tend to enhance achievement. Additonal support for the positive effects of democratic parent-child relationships is provided by G. Weigard (1957) in his study of 17 successful and 17 unsuccessful students possessing comparable ability. Weigard's successful group reported less stringent parental supervision of leisure time activities, greater encouragement by parents toward success in work and play and a generally more positive atmosphere at home. Similar findings were reported by J. V. Pierce (1961) in his study of tenth- and twelfth-grade boys. Pierce found that mothers of his high-achieving boys received lower scores on authoritarian measures.

Other investigators, most notably E. M. Drews and J. E. Teaham (1957), have reported that authoritarian dispositions of parents have enhanced, rather than impeded, achievement. Drews and Teaham found mothers of high achievers to be more authoritarian in their treatment of their children. The academically successful child was characterized as one who has a rigidly designed place at home, which he is expected to keep with docile acceptance. High achievers' parents conveyed the impression that they know what is best for their children and these standards are rarely questioned.

Conflicting results have been reported by investigators concerning the effects of broken homes on academic achievement. For instance, Joanne Veroff et al. (1960) and C. Sutcliffe (1958) state that high achievers more frequently lived with both parents and possess feelings of happiness in regard to home, parents, attitude, and friends; whereas underachievers tend to come from broken homes or from homes where there are weak ties between parents. On the other end of the continuum, E. C. Clark (1961), in his study of personal data cards of 94 underachievers in the Independence, Missouri, junior high school system, found that 81 percent of the underachievers lived with both parents.

Most investigators report that parents play the most important and most essential role in the development of the self-concept and achievement motivation. Self-concept emerges first and affects achievement; as a consequence, it may either enhance or impede achievement motivation. Parent-child relationships—whether they be authoritarian or democratic—affect the achievement pattern of the child.

Peers

Peer relationships, though important for all preadolescents and adolescents, appear to be of particular importance to underachievers. For instance, Morrow and Wilson (1961), in their study of bright achieving and bright underachieving high school boys, found that underachievers tended to be socially anchored in a peer clique society, and described themselves as belonging to cliques which possessed negative social attitudes. Similar results are reported by J. S. Coleman (1961), who found that achievement ranked low as a criterion for admission into leading groups in the high schools that he studied. Being smart or making good grades ranked sixth in a list comprised of eight criteria. Only 12 percent of the boys and girls felt that school success was important for social acceptance in leading groups. Academic achievement apparently is not a prerequisite for peer acceptance. Underachievers are generally socially competent and are as readily accepted by peers as are achievers and overachievers.

Self-Esteem and Learning Disability

The issue of learning disabilities in childhood and youth has attracted considerable attention in recent years (e.g., Cruickshank 1977; Hobbs 1975; Kephart 1960; Wiederholt 1974). I, too, surveyed 200 specialists in the field of learning disabilities (1978). Demographic data gathered in the survey are summarized in Table 5.1.

The data presented in Table 5.1 are generally consistent with those reported elsewhere, that the majority of learning-disabled children come from middle-class homes and possess average ability. Boys outnumber girls three to one, and the typical learning-disabled child is approximately two years behind in reading and arithmetic and is at least one year behind in grade placement.

Children experiencing learning problems tend to esteem themselves lower than their counterparts who do not have learning problems (Battle 1979). I studied 134 boys and 53 girls enrolled in grades one to seven and found that children experiencing learning problems earned lower self-esteem and perception of ability scores than comparable children who were making satisfactory academic progress (1979). Findings from the study are summarized in Table 5.2.

ENHANCING

TABLE 5.1. Demographic Features Derived from a Survey of Clinicians Working with Children with Learning Disabilities. (N = 861).

IQ		Reading		Arithmetic		Socio-Status		Class		Age		Sex	
Score	%	Grade	%	Grade	%	Level	%	Grade	%	Range	%	Boys %	Girls %
70–79	10	–2	32	–2	10	Upper	17	–K	1	4–7	3	76	24
80–89	13	2–5	33	2–5	51	Up./Md.	18	1–6	45	8–12	43		
90–109	54	5–8	25	5–8	29	Middle	35	7–9	39	13–15	40		
110–119	20	8–10	4	8–10	10	Low./Md.	15	10–12	15	16–18	14		
120–129	2	10–12	6	10–12	0	Lower	15	12–	0				

TABLE 5.2. *Means, Standard Deviations, Correlations, and Significance for Normal and Learning-Disabled Students.*

		Self-Esteem			Perception-of-Ability		
Group	N	Mean	S.D.	p	Mean	S.D.	p
Normal	97	36.44	8.19	.001	47.47	11.39	.001
Learning-Disabled	90	30.23	7.59	0	35.33	11.11	0

Data presented in Table 5.2 indicate that children with learning problems scored significantly lower than those who did not have learning problems. These data indicate that children who are experiencing academic difficulties at school perceive their worth and ability to achieve lower than do students who are apparently making satisfactory academic progress. The findings presented in Table 5.2 are consistent with those of M. C. Shaw's research group (1960), who found that more successful students tend to evaluate their worth more positively. Additional support is provided by my study (1975) in which we found that students who were experiencing academic or behavioral problems earned self-esteem scores that were significantly lower that those of students who were functioning satisfactorily.

Children with learning problems, in addition to possessing lower self-esteem, also tend to possess a greater degree of brain dysfunction. Findings from a study of the incidence of brain dysfunction in learning-disabled and normal children, conducted by our research group (1980), are presented in Table 5.3.

TABLE 5.3. *Incidence of Brain Dysfunction in Normal and Learning-Disabled Students.*

		Diagnostic Classification (%)			Self-Esteem	
Group	N	Dys-functional	Nearly Normal	Normal	Mean	S.D.
Normal	65	13.8	33.8	52.3	39.40	6.94
Learning-Disabled	67	92.6	7.4	—	35.59	8.30

Data presented in Table 5.3 indicate that children with learning problems experience a greater degree of biological dysfunctioning than those who are making satisfactory academic progress. These children (learning disabled) also earn lower self-esteem scores.

ENHANCING

Summary

Psychologists generally support the proposition that achievement is significantly related to self-esteem. There is also considerable agreement concerning the ineffectiveness of current educational procedures and techniques for enhancing self-esteem and subsequently achievement. Consequently, we have the underachiever, the student whose academic performance is considerably lower than his assessed potential. These youngsters (underachievers) represent 15 to 50 percent of all students in North American school systems. More boys than girls are identified as being underachievers, and underachievement in boys usually commences earlier than it does in girls. The syndrome of underachievement usually commences during the elementary years and escalates and continues throughout the junior and senior high school years.

Underachievers tend to possess lower self-esteem, more hostility, more negative attitudes toward school and generally lower levels of adjustment than their achieving and overachieving counterparts. The etiology of underachievement is multivariant; as a consequence, it is often difficult to determine precisely what is the underlying cause of the underachievement. Researchers who have studied the problem generally agree that underachievement is a serious problem which affects many North American children and youth. These authorities feel that there is a critical need for educators to become more effective in their ability to assist pupils who are underachieving. Underachievement, admittedly, is a complex problem and currently there are no clear-cut means of resolving it. In Chapter 6, however, we will present some hypotheses regarding the underachievement syndrome and offer suggestions on how this problem may be dealt with.

ENHANCING

6

SELF-ESTEEM AND READING

A number of programs for teaching reading to children in general, and to slow or non-readers in particular, have emerged in recent years. For example, the *Distar Language Development Program*, which has proved to be successful with some children, failed significantly to alter the ever-growing problem of reading deficiency. The *Distar* program does not stand alone. No program has been universally effective in alleviating the problem of reading disability. It therefore appears, at least from my point of view, that we have been expending our energies in the wrong directions. We have been overly concerned with methodology and techniques and have frequently overlooked the child himself, his feelings, desires, attitudes, and perceptions of self. We have often failed to realize that most children do not fail because they lack potential to succeed, but rather because they refuse to learn. These children are experiencing what is called "failure-to-achieve syndrome," a pathological condition characterized by self-defeating patterns which include under-achievement, deviant behavior, and apathy and negativism which are accompanied by low self-esteem. Thus, exposure to special reading programs or remedial programs will not work successfully unless we first attend to and resolve the basic problem at hand: the student's failure-to-achieve disposition. Once the issue has been resolved and the child has reevaluated his perceptions of self and is able to view himself in a favorable fashion, academic progress can be made at a rapid pace. In this chapter we review the relationship between self-esteem and reading, and attempt to illustrate how closely interrelated these two variables are.

Most professionals in education know that there is a positive relationship between self-esteem and reading; and this position is generally supported by data derived from the literature. For instance, Quandt (1973), in his review of literature dealing with the relationship between reading and self-perceptions, concluded that a positive self-concept contributes greatly to a child's reading ability. D. D. Lumpkin (1959), in his study of the relationship between self-concept and achievement, identified two groups of fifth-grade subjects. The groups identified in the study were comprised of 24 overachievers in reading and 24 underachievers in reading. These boys and girls, who were matched for chronological age, mental age, sex, and socioeconomic background, were administered a self-concept scale; the data derived form self-concept scores indicate that overachievers possess more positive self-concepts than underachievers. Additional support for this position is provided by W. B. Brookover, T. Sailor, and A. Paterson (1964), who tested 1,050 seventh-grade students and selected 110 over- and underachievers from this group to study more extensively. Findings from their study revealed a significant, positive relationship between self-concept of ability and grade-point average. Similar findings are presented by Toller (1967) who studied achieving and retarded readers and found that retarded readers felt less adequate and less secure in their relationships with peers and adults. They also reported low self-concepts and felt that they were encountering more and greater problems than their achieving counterparts. M. Bruck and R. F. Bodwin (1962), in their study of 30 third-, sixth-, and seventh-grade youngsters who were underachieving in reading, found a positive and significant relationship between reading disability and a negative self-concept. R. L. Williams and S. Cole (1968), in their study of 80 sixth-grade students, found a positive and significant correlation between self-concept and reading achievement. These investigators concluded that a child's perception of school is closely related to his conception of self.

Reading achievement also appears to be related to one's perception of ability. For example, M. H. Jason and B. Dubnow (1973), in their study of 231 fifth-grade students, found a significant relationship between self-perceptions of reading abilities and actual achievement in reading.

Self-concept also appears to be related to other disabilities as well. Support for this position is provided by R. F. Bodwin (1959), who studied 300 students in grades three and six, and identified three equal groups of subjects: 100 with a reading disability, 100 with an arithmetic disability, and 100 with no disability. Findings from Bodwin's study revealed a positive, significant correlation between immature self-concept and both reading and arithmetic disability.

Reading and Maladjustment

Adequate achievement in reading is essential for the child's feelings of well-being, and appears to be highly related to healthy personality adjustment. Failure in reading thus impedes a child's personal development and lowers his self-esteem, as it relates to himself and others as well. A number of writers (e.g., Gates 1941; Knapp 1959; and Dechant 1968) state that a circular pattern of behavior develops when the child continually experiences failure in reading. For instance, E. Dechant (1968) states:

> The relationship between reading disability and emotional and social maladjustment frequently is circular in mature. Early reading failure leads to maladjustment and personal maladjustment in turn prevents further growth in reading. It is quite conceivable that in certain cases reading failure and personal maladjustment have their own distinct causes. Generally, if the reading failure is emotional in nature, the child will have difficulties in other academic areas also. If the emotional problem was caused by failure in reading, the emotional difficulty is reduced when the child learns to read (p. 71).

Further support for the position which assumes that reading disability is associated with personal maladjustment is provided by A. I. Gates (1941), Berkowitz and Rothman (1955), Dechant (1968), N. B. Smith (1955), Knapp (1959), A. J. Fraiser and A. W. Combs (1958), and G. D. Spache (1957).

A. I. Gates (1941), one of the earliest theorists to report on the relationship between reading disability and personal adjustment, stated:

> All of these symptoms or forms of nervousness, withdrawal, aggression, defeatism, and chronic worry appear among cases in which maladjustment is the cause, the result, or the concomitant of reading disability. It is therefore not possible to tell whether they were causes or effects or an accompaniment of trouble in reading (p. 79).

Berkowitz and Rothman (1955) made similar comments when they stated:

> Whatever the outward manifestation of the maladjustment, the most obvious result is a history of scholastic failure, even when intellectually the child is adequate and should have succeeded .... Emotional maladjustment can cause academic retardation, and academic retardation can contribute considerably to a child's emotional problems (p. 66).

Research findings indicate that children who are disabled readers tend to view themselves negatively and as being unable to learn; whereas youngsters who are successful readers tend to view themselves positively and see themselves as being capable of learning and generally place great value on reading. Support for this proposition is provided by Dechant (1968), who states:

> Studies show that the incidence of maladjustment among poor readers is greater than among good readers. It is not always easy to establish whether personality maladjustment is the cause, the effect, or a concomitant circumstance .... Educational malfunctions, most commonly those of reading, signify emotional problems (p. 70).

N. B. Smith, reporting in 1955, noted that research reveals that there is a high incidence of emotional disturbance among children retarded in reading, and that emotional disturbance may cause reading difficulties, or vice versa, both usually being the result of a constellation of causes (p. 10). Similar observations are reported by George D. Spache (1957) who stated:

> The handicapped readers are, as a group, inclined to be more aggressive and defensive than children of their ages, less self-insightful, and are relatively poor in knowing how to handle situations of conflict with adults. They tend to exhibit a passive, but defensive, attitude or negativism toward authority figures. In fact, their total adjustment to adults is decidedly poorer and unlike children of their age group (p. 466).

Knapp (1955), in his text entitled *Guidance in the Elementary School*, stressed the role that reading plays in personal adjustment when he wrote:

> Reading is basic to the successful adjustment of the child in school and life. His whole pattern of behavior in and out of school may be altered sharply by how well he learns to read and to read effectively .... It may affect his attitudes, viewpoints, interests, and understanding about other people of the world .... The child's ability to read seems to be closely interwoven with his total personality development. Maladjustment may occur if the child is not taught to read

according to his particular needs and differences (p. 192).

The failure-to-achieve syndrome, which is experienced by an increasingly large number of youngsters, is not due to lack of potential; rather, it is a consequence of problems in adjustment generally associated with low self-esteem. This position is reflected in the writing of Fraiser and Combs (1958), who state that most failures in reading and spelling are not results of the incapacity of the student; rather, they are symptoms of his attitude toward the tasks of reading and spelling. He sees himself inadequately, so he behaves inadequately. Additional support for the position is provided by Combs (1958), who states that most children who come to reading clinics, cannot read because they believe they cannot read and believe themselves to be unable. They behave in terms of the concepts they possess (p. 315).

Teacher Influence on Self-Perceptions and Reading Achievement

Some investigators have reported that pupils' perceptions of teachers' feelings toward them affects their self-perceptions and achievement. For instance, Helen H. Davidson and D. Lang (1960) studied 203 proficient readers enrolled in grades four, five, and six, and found that subjects' perceptions of their teachers' feelings toward them correlated positively and significantly with perception of self. They also found a positive relationship between favorable perceptions of teachers' feelings and academic achievement and, in turn classroom behavior. J. M. Pahordy (1969) states that teachers' feelings toward children will subsequently affect the child's ability to read. He suggests that this occurs in three steps:

1. A teacher believes a child will succeed or fail; she communicates this belief, either verbally or nonverbally, to the child.
2. The child begins to see himself as the teacher sees him.
3. The child's perceptions of his reading abilities are reinforced by association with actual performance.

Additional support for the position that teachers' perceptions affects pupils' perception of self is provided by H. V. Perkins (1958), who studied fourth- and sixth-grade students and their teachers, and found that teachers' perceptions of children's self-concepts show a positive and significant relationship to the children's expressed self-concepts. Snygg and Combs (1959) in their text, entitled *Individual Behavior*, in discussing the role of the teacher in the development of the self-image, stated:

> The learning of any skill of item of subject matter is accompanied by the formation of attitudes by the pupil towards the subject, towards school, towards his teacher, towards teachers in general, towards adults, towards society, and towards himself which may be desirable or undesirable. As a result, how the subject matter is taught may be even more important than what is taught (p. 240).

The importance of the role the teacher plays in the development and maintenance of the self is vividly illustrated by J. W. Staines (1958) in his study of the responses and comments of classroom teachers and the influences that these responses and comments have on the self-concepts of their children. He hypothesized:

1. The self-concept is a learned structure growing mainly from comments made by other people and from inferences drawn by children out of their experiences in home, school, and other social groups.
2. Consequently, teachers could make marked differences in the self-concepts

of children with their comments on the child's performance, status, and self-confidence.

Staines analyzed the responses and comments of a group of teachers and found that students with teachers who used democratic methods, made positive comments, and gave consideration to the child's self-concept, made positive changes in self-concepts of their children; whereas marked psychological insecurity and maladjustment were found in the children whose teachers emphasized correctness and subject matter. Teachers who emphasized correctness and subject matter did not recognize the important role that perceptions of self play in the educational process. Staines made the following comments in his discussion of the implications of his findings:

> The educational significance of the self is reaffirmed when it is realized that changes in the self picture are an inevitable part of both outcomes and conditions of learning in every classroom, whether or not the teacher is aware of them . . . . It is clear that teaching methods can be adapted so that definite changes of the sought will occur in the self. The self can be deliberately produced by suitable teaching methods (p. 109).

The classroom teacher becomes the most "significant other" in the development of the child's self-concept after he reaches school age. This assumption is supported by Labenne and Green (1969), who stressed the important role that teachers play in the formation of children's self-concepts when they stated:

> Any person who is intimately involved in the administration of rewards and punishments is in a position to become a significant other. It is not merely the ability or responsibility of administering the system . . . that makes a teacher a significant other. Rather it is the manner in which he uses his authority that causes him to have a potent impact (p. 27).

Self-Esteem: An Antecedent of Reading Achievement

Although some investigators (e.g., Williams 1968; Ruhly 1971) argue that there is no significant relationship between self-esteem and reading, the majority of theorists support the position that there is a definite, positive, significant relationship between self-esteem and reading. A number of theorists have taken this position a step further, and argue that a positive self-concept is an antecedent to achievement in reading. For instance, E. Gann (1945) in his book entitled *Reading Difficulty and Personality Organization,* states that poor perceptions of self are antecedents of reading disabilities, and that these negative perceptions of self are not caused by difficulties in school, but are brought by the child to the school. Support for this position is provided by W. M. Wattenberg and Clare Clifford (1964), who assessed the self-concept and ego strength of kindergarten children and two and one half years later related these measures to reading achievement and found that the concept of self is an antecedent to and is predictive of reading disability. Lamy (1964) in her study of 52 first-grade students found a positive relationship between a child's perception of himself and his world while in kindergarten and subsequent achievement in reading in first grade. She concluded that self-concept and perceptions of the environment may be causal factors in reading achievement.

If a positive self-concept is an antecedent of achievement, it appears worthwhile, then, to expose young children to activities (e.g., in kindergarten) designed to enhance self-esteem, which will in turn facilitate achievement. Support for early intervention is provided by data derived from a number of studies. For example, Givliani (1968) with the above assumption in mind, studied 366 kindergarten boys and girls, and found a significant positive relationship between self-concept and reading readiness. If self-esteem and reading readiness are significantly related, and if we accept the proposition that a positive self-concept is an antecedent of reading achievement, it seems appropriate to intervene at an early age and attempt to enhance the self-concept of children; this should, in turn, enhance reading achievement.

Remediation and Reading Achievement

Research findings indicate that there is a need for the development and implementation of programs that will enhance self-esteem and subsequently achievement. Most programs, heretofore, however, unfortunately, have not been effective in providing the kind of assistance youngsters need. The lack of success of such programs is brilliantly illustrated by R. Dreikurs, Bernice B. Grunwald, and F. C. Pepper (1971), in their text entitled *Maintaining Sanity in the Classroom*, in which they presented the following cases of children who made no progress in reading in spite of years of remedial help, but subsequently learned how to read in a short period of time after their anti-learning tendency was removed and once their self-image was changed:

Case Report 6.1.

Peter was an only child of elderly parents. He was small and underweight until the age of four. Both parents constantly worried about him and gave-in to him in order not to upset him. When he could not have his way, Peter screamed and threw anything that was near at his parents. When they gave-in to him, "he was lovable" and very affectionate—which both parents adored.

Peter was not sent to kindergarten. The parents were afraid that he might catch diseases from the other children. They were equally afraid to let him go out and play with other children. One of them took him to the park every afternoon, where he would sit on a swing while a parent pushed it. The mother insisted that Peter loved it that way, since he never asked to be allowed to play with other children.

When Peter entered first grade, he cried and would not let go of his mother. She promised to stand outside where he could see her through the window. After some time, the teacher insisted that the mother go away, which she did, only to wait for Peter around the corner. She brought him to school and picked him up at noon and in the afternoon every day for two years in spite of the teachers' appeal to allow the boy to walk home alone or with other children. Peter made no progress in the first grade and had to repeat the grade. This seemed to have no effect on him or his parents.

At the end of the second year, he was promoted to grade two, although he had not learned any more than during the first year. Thus, he was promoted again into third grade. Here he spent most of his time either at the window or going back and forth to the washroom or to the drinking fountain. He seemed not to hear when the teacher spoke to him.

While still in the third grade, Peter's mother had a fatal accident. This changed his entire life. The father worked during the day; he left the house before Peter had to leave for school. They couldn't afford a housekeeper, and Peter was forced to shift for himself. He had to walk to school either by himself or with other children. After school, he waited for his father in the home of a neighbor who had young children.

The first weeks were indeed pitiful. Peter was too stunned, or else he understood that tantrums would not help him. He walked as if in a sleep. For a while, the children in the class overprotected him. They took him to the cafeteria where they sat with him, they walked him from and to school, and they invited him to their homes to wait for his father. Gradually, he formed relationships with them, and he discovered that he could hold his own quite successfully. This change carried over into his attitude toward everything that concerned school and school activities. By the end of the school year he could read and write as well as many of the students in the class.

Case Report 6.2.

Percy was the younger of two children. His parents were divorced when he was three years old. Each parent took one child; Percy remained with his mother. Percy's mother ran a small grocery store where he spent each day. He was a very fearful child, afraid of lightning and thunder, the dark, animals, and strange people. He refused to ride a tricycle because he might fall off. He slept in the same bed with his mother until he was eleven, when she was helped to understand she was holding him back with her overprotection.

Percy's school attendance was most irregular. Usually he skipped mornings, but often did not show up for many days in a row. In class, he was generally well behaved and showed considerable interest and knowledge in science. He lacked the most rudimentary reading skills. Whatever he learned in his remedial reading class, he forgot within minutes.

When Percy was eleven years old, his mother became alarmed about his reading disability, and she came to the teacher for help. This was unusual for this woman because she had never kept any appointments with teachers of any grade. The mother was helped to understand how she had deprived Percy of normal development by making him the center of her life, by giving in to him, by serving him as though he was incapable of learning to be responsible for himself. She was helped to see the connection between what she did and school retardation. She was an intelligent woman and desperate enough to follow the teacher's advice. It was a difficult task for all of them—the mother, Percy, and the teacher. Although Percy was prepared for the changes that would take place at home, he threw tantrums, broke dishes, refused to go to school, and so forth. The mother, desperate, ran to the teacher for help almost daily. Her biggest difficulty was in knowing how to show love and affection for the boy without being his slave. Both of them required frequent counseling—the mother by the teacher, and Percy by the teacher and through frequent reassurance by the group. In this way, both of them were reeducated and slowly formed a new relationship. Percy's school attendance became regular, and he began to form social interrelationships with some of the children. The teacher assigned him to lead the Christmas play. This required the memorization of lines. Percy had to depend on other children to read the lines to him, which he did; but in the process he developed a feeling for reading for the first time; reading seemed to make sense and he could see the need for it. It was then that the remedial instruction that he had received for over two years took on importance and meaning. He progressed rapidly.

Case Report 6.3.

Jerry was classified as a non-learner after four years of individual instruction. At age eleven he still looked like eight, and people who did not know his age would often ask him if he were in the first or second grade. He never answered such questions, but hung his head or looked away. Whenever he was confronted with such a question in front of his mother, she would quickly reply that he was in the fifth grade, which was not true, and she added that he was very shy. Jerry was the second child of five children. His older brother died when he was three years old. The other siblings were born when he was five and already in kindergarten. After his brother's death, the parents doubled their vigilance and protection, not only of this boy, but of all their children. Jerry was kept at home on rainy days. He was never allowed to join his class on field trips or in energetic activities in the gymnasium. In class, he was very talkative, but in a sly, underhanded manner. When the teacher looked at him, he assumed an angelic expression, but the moment she took her eyes off him he started talking to his neighbors. Usually, he brought some object to show off or to play with under his desk.

Whenever the teacher called on him, he got up in a daze. He hung his head so low that it would almost touch his desk. He often remained in this position in spite of the teacher's invitation to sit down. The children looked at him with pity, and those nearby often pleaded with him to sit down.

Jerry could never find his scissors. His desk was crammed with unwritten papers and with various objects he brought from home. He could neither read nor write, and he showed no interest in any subject. Whenever the teacher tried to help him, he shook his head and mumbled, "I can't." Nevertheless, Jerry never missed going to the remedial class; he never had to be reminded. During an interview with the mother, it became obvious that the parents accepted the belief that Jerry was retarded mentally as well as physically, and that he needed their protection. It was impossible to persuade these parents to try a different approach. They were convinced of Jerry's retardation and reproached themselves for having children, as one of the father's brothers was mentally retarded and in an institution. They blamed Jerry's condition on heredity.

During one of the class discussions, it was brought up that sometimes it "pays" for children to play "dumb" even though they are quite intelligent. Jerry, who had never taken an obvious interest in those discussions, raised his hand for the first time. He asked that we explain what one could possibly get out of playing dumb. He said, "If your dumb, you're dumb. You don't play like you are dumb because you get nothing." The group disagreed with him and gave him many examples how it pays off for someone to play dumb, how people are forced into their service, how nobody expects anything of such children, and how they get out of assuming responsibilities for themselves. One child said that it may pay off while one is young, but when one grows up, such a person will have a hard time because he won't know how to do anything for himself. Nobody mentioned Jerry's name, but he suddenly got up and announced in a clear voice, "But I'm not playing dumb." The teacher asked him to explain this comment; but all he said was, "I'm not playing," over and over. For several seconds one could hear a pin drop. Nobody said a word, but everyone looked at Jerry. Finally, one girl remarked "How do you know, Jerry? Maybe you're smarter than you think, but you never try to find out. You don't even try to walk home by yourself like other kids."

After class was dismissed, Jerry stopped at the teacher's desk and timidly asked if she could speak to his parents and ask them to allow him to come to and walk from school by himself. This was Jerry's first step toward independence. After he learned to walk to school by himself, he asked to be permitted to walk in the park by himself. Next, the teacher induced his parents to get him an alarm clock and let him get up in the morning and get ready for school by himself. Each time Jerry made the slightest progress, the parents were instructed to show appreciation. In class, the children complimented Jerry and showed their interest in all of his achievements. As parents' and children's attitudes toward him changed, so did his self-evaluation. When asked a question, he know longer hung his head; he answered without fear. He did not always know the answers, but he showed no sign of fear or shame. Jerry's school progress was unbelievably fast. His dormant ambition now came to fore, and he set high goals for himself, like completing a reader in a month. He did. At the end of the year, he had successfully covered three years of work.

Each of the children presented in the case studies listed here, had been exposed to remedial reading programs which had little success in modifying reading ability until a change in perception of self occurred. A reevaluation of self-worth is an essential prerequisite which must be firmly established if we are to successfully remediate reading disabilities and foster achievement in reading.

Research data substantiate the empirical observation which holds that remedial reading programs (e.g., resource rooms, adaptation classes, etc.) which have been implemented in the past, have generally been ineffective and have typically failed to reduce significantly the discrepancy between potential and actual reading skills. It seems appropriate that we explore the area of reading more extensively and develop programs that will *work*. What we need are programs that take into account the *whole* individual, which are not merely concerned with reading techniques, but also have mechanisms built in that are designed to improve the child's emotional status in general and his self-esteem specifically.

If we accept the position which holds that self-esteem is an antecedent of reading, we would assume that modification of self-perceptions (especially perceptions of ability to achieve) must be made before remedial instruction begins and throughout the instructional program. Support for this position is provided by findings from a study I conducted in which we analyzed the self-reports of deviant and nondeviant students. "Deviant" students were defined as being those children who were referred to the school psychologist by their teachers for academic, behavioral, or emotional reasons; whereas "nondeviant" students were defined as those youngsters who were never referred to the school psychologists for any reason. Subjects in the two groups were equated in accordance to grade placement, age, sex, and socioeconomic status. Findings of the study are presented in Table 6.1.

The data presented in Table 6.1 indicate that nondeviant subjects scored significantly higher in all areas of self-esteem that deviant subjects. Results indicate quite strongly that feelings of self-worth are associated with achievement and levels of adjustment. Findings indicate quite clearly that students who are experiencing difficulties in the school environment (and as a result, are subsequently referred to their school psychologist) generally tend to evaluate their personal worth significantly lower than students who are apparently functioning adequately within the school environment. These findings are consistent with the position taken by M. C. Shaw's group (1960), who argue that students who evaluate themselves highly are the ones who generally tend to experience a greater degree of success in the academic environment.

TABLE 6.1. *Means, Standard Deviations, and Significance for Deviant and Nondeviant Students.*

| | Deviant | | Nondeviant | | |
Subscale	Mean	S.D.	Mean	S.D.	*p*
Total	26.35	7.97	33.16	7.29	.001
General	13.89	4.46	17.12	4.41	.001
Social	4.69	2.01	5.71	1.51	.001
Parents	4.64	2.13	5.53	1.96	.001
School	3.08	1.95	4.91	1.89	.001

Why Children Don't Read

Findings from numerous studies have indicated that a growing number of children fail to read at grade level. These findings have been the basic reason for the emergence of numerous theories in recent years which have attempted to explain "Why Johnny can't read." Some theorists argue that children experience difficulties in reading because they are deprived, disadvantaged, or come from lower socioeconomic environments. Others state that disabled readers have been exposed to limited experiential environments and as a consequence are culturally and perceptually deprived. There are also those who state that poor readers have minimal brain damage or that they are experiencing some form of neurological dysfunctioning. John Money (1966), in his reaction to the latter position, states that it is fashionable today to talk of "minimal brain damage" in relation to reading disabilities, and this really is begging the question. In the majority of cases, no kind of brain damage can be demonstrated by today's techniques. EEGs do not support the hypothesis of minimal brain damage in retarded readers. There are minor EEG anomalies, but the same are seen in children with or without diagnosis. They merely indicate a maturation anomaly. Disability, specifically with respect to reading, is rare in cases of brain pathology in childhood (p. 33).

In a similar vein, L. Eisenberg (1966) states, "Competent investigators have been led to contrary conclusions about the role of handedness, heredity, perceptual handicap, and the like. Incomplete cerebral dominance does not account for reading problems. The determination of laterality is not so simply a matter as what was once thought, nor is brainedness so readily to be inferred from handedness" (p. 8). Other experts state that children cannot read because they were not prepared properly at home, in kindergarten, or in first grade. None of the theories just listed, however, has been satisfactory in delineating why so many youngsters are disabled readers.

Dreikurs, Grunwald, and Pepper (1971) make an interesting observation concerning reading when they suggest that psychological factors play a major role in reading. These writers state that remedial techniques for enhancing reading skills have been basically ineffective because they have not been directed towards the child's negative attitudes—those attitudes which he possesses toward himself, in general, and reading, specifically. Corrective efforts, therefore, must be concerned with changing the child's perceptions and attitudes if they are to be effective in facilitating reading skills. The Dreikurs group states that remedial teaching requires not merely a specific teaching technique; it must be directed toward changing some deeper psychological dynamics of the child, stimulating a change in motivation. Instead of involving the child in the laborious practice of reading, the teacher has to assume corrective functions of a psychological nature (p. 222).

Dreikurs, Grunwald, and Pepper offer the following advice concerning remediation and reading:

1. The teacher cannot ignore the faulty values on which the child may operate, like the fallacy of constantly comparing himself to others, of being more concerned with success than with learning. Such distorted ambition often leads to the assumption of being a failure. The child may need a better concept of order and usefulness. The teacher can and should enhance the child's comprehension of social living. Such teaching should not be incidental to the practice of reading, but rather to the essence of remedial teaching. This can be achieved through individual and particularly group discussion, since most students in remedial classes share similar deficiencies in their value systems.

2. The basis for effective educational endeavors is a proper interpersonal relationship. Children in need of special instruction have not been able to establish such a relationship in their families. Otherwise, they would not be academically and socially deficient. The teacher will be put in the same role of mother, father, and other authority figures played in the child's family unless he or she makes deliberate efforts to recognize such faulty patterns and to correct them. This conclusion of "adults-against-the-child" is fortified if the teacher tries to involve the mother in supervising reading.

3. The teacher has to be free from the assumption that the difficulty in reading permits any conclusion about the reading ability of the child. Presently, the real ability of children in this regard is grossly underestimated by the majority of teachers.

4. Children *will not* learn, rather than *cannot* learn. The child is opposing and sabotaging efforts at instruction. Corrective efforts must be aimed at this unwillingness to learn, although the child may display a pretended desire to cover up his real intention. "The mind of such a child is full of resistance and must be emptied, in contrast to the prevalent opinion that his mind is empty waiting to be filled" (p. 5).

Research findings indicate that children who fail to read generally do not fail because they lack potential; rather, because they are subject to emotional factors in which low self-esteem plays a major role. Failure to read or achieve in general is usually a manifestation of the child's inability to deal with hostility he possesses toward parents. The youngster's refusal to achieve is his way of "getting back" at parents he feels have rejected, belittled, and demeaned him. The child may retaliate against parents in many ways; but failure-to-achieve is one of the most popular tactics the young child employs in his attempts to cause pain to parents. If the child refuses to achieve, it usually results in the parents having to come to the school to meet with principals, school psychologists, counselors and teachers to discuss their child's lack of progress. These meetings usually evoke guilt, conflicts, hostilities, and frustrations in parents. Parents, in addition to personal injury, usually have to suffer financially as well. For example, they frequently provide lucrative sums of money for private tutoring that generally does not work. The most profound punishment for parents, however, occurs when they have to face the reality that their child is not living up to their expectations, which prompts many of the parents to ask the question, "Why is he doing this to us?" The child's behavior (failure to achieve), though it generally causes a certain degree of grief for parents, is nevertheless self-defeating; and the child himself always suffers the most. The failure-to-achieve syndrome is illustrated in the following summaries.

Case Report 6.4.

Jamie was a thirteen-year-old youngster who was the second child in a family comprised of three boys and one girl. His father was a prominent physician, and his mother was active in community affairs. Jamie was small for his age and always found it difficult to keep pace with his older brother. He experienced academic difficulties as early as second grade, but did not fail until seventh grade, because his father and mother insisted that he be promoted each year and that his difficulties were caused by insensitive teachers who employed ineffective teaching methods and were lacking in their concerns for Jamie's needs. Jamie's seventh-grade teachers, nevertheless, insisted that he repeat the grade; and they stood firm in spite of parental opposition. Jamie continued his nonachievement pattern during his second year in seventh grade and continued to insist that he could not do the work because it was too difficult. Jamie was subsequently referred to the school psychologist who found him to be a bright youngster who possessed high average intelligence. His Verbal IQ score was 107, Performance IQ 115, and Full Scale score was 112 on the WISC-R. Personality testing revealed that Jamie resented his father and possessed a great deal of fear of him. His self-esteem was low, and he felt that his parents did not feel that he was good enough.

The school psychologist arranged an interview for the parents and teachers at the school, and discussed and interpreted test findings. Jamie's fears and repressed hostilities were discussed; and the parents, especially the father, were made aware of the reasons for Jamie's lack of achievement. For instance, it was disclosed that Jamie's hostilities were due to feelings of rejection he was experiencing, as a result of his belief that his father preferred his older, more successful brother over him. Jamie struck back by refusing to achieve, which was his way of punishing parents who, he felt, had rejected him. The parents did not really accept this theory, but were so desperate that they agreed to accept the recommendations and to communicate to Jamie overtly and otherwise that they cared as much for him as they did for their other children. Jamie was somewhat skeptical; and progress initially was quite slow; but he finally became convinced that his parents were sincere. He subsequently reassessed his relationship with his parents, and his achievement, in turn, reflected this reevaluation. He successfully completed seventh grade, and follow-up two years later revealed that he had continued to achieve at a rate that was consistent with his potential.

Case Report 6.5.

Bobby was an eleven-year-old who was the youngest child of elderly parents. His three sisters and brothers ranged in age from twenty-two to eighteen. Bobby made As and Bs in grades one through five, but was failing sixth grade. School officials had invited Bobby's parents to school on several occasions to discuss his academic progress. The parents, especially the mother, insisted that Bobby's lack of achievement was a consequence of poor teaching and that the school was responsible for his academic difficulties. School officials responded similarly and stated that Bobby was a pampered child who simply refused to do his work; and that if he did not improve significantly, he would fail sixth grade. The parents responded by insisting that Bobby be assessed by an outside, more objective source. School officials somewhat reluctantly agreed to adhere to the parents request and referred Bobby to the school psychologist before making a final decision to fail him. Intellectual testing revealed that Bobby's Verbal, Performance, and Full Scale IQ scores on the WISC-R were 124, 121, and 126, respectively. Personality test results indicated that he was a fairly withdrawn individual who possessed low self-esteem and was experiencing considerable difficulties adjusting in the home and school environments. An interview was scheduled for Bobby's parents at the school, but only the mother attended. It became apparent shortly after the interview began that the mother was a domineering individual who imposed her standards on other family members and ran the household in a very authoritarian fashion. Test findings were interpreted to the mother, and she was told that Bobby's underachievement was his way of rebelling against impositions at home, which he had subsequently generalized to other adults (teachers) in the school environment. She was told that Bobby found it difficult to verbalize his objections to these impositions, so he chose a more subtle way (underachieving) of communicating his unhappiness about these restrictions.

School officials were informed that Bobby's negative behavior at school was a consequence of generalization of feelings which emanated in the home environment. The mother and school officials were encouraged to "bury the hatchet" and to respond in a more democratic fashion toward Bobby, recognizing his needs and respecting his desire for autonomy. The mother and teachers were encouraged to let Bobby make his own decisions concerning achievement. They were also instructed to communicate to him that he was a bright individual who had the potential to achieve highly, but that it was his right to achieve or not: Regardless of whether he achieved or not, he would be accepted and respected as an individual who has rights, and is as worthy as any other individual.

This approach was implemented at home and at school; and shortly afterward (approximately three weeks) a dramatic change was observed in Bobby. He reevaluated his worth as an individual, became more cooperative at school, and his academic achievement increased significantly. He completed sixth grade handily and enrolled in an academically oriented junior high school that caters to bright, high-achieving students.

Case Report 6.6.

Johnny was a fifteen-year-old, only child, whose mother had married for the third time. Johnny's mother and father separated when he was nine years old, and he was referred to the school psychologist initially several months after this break-up. At this time, he was making minimal academic progress, and was a fairly severe disciplinary problem at school. For example, he refused to turn in assignments, would "act out" in class, and refused to cooperate with teachers.

Numerous techniques were tried by the school psychologist and teachers, but nothing seemed to work. Johnny nevertheless was promoted each year, despite his poor performance. He was re-referred to the school psychologist when he was in ninth grade for the same reasons mentioned earlier. The school psychologist found him to be a fairly bright youngster who was not experiencing any significant degree of psychopathology. His WISC-R IQ scores placed him within the average range of ability, and his overall adjustment was fairly satisfactory.

An interview was arranged for the parents, but only the mother attended. She was a fairly timid individual who readily admitted that she had tried everything she could think of over the years with Johnny, but that nothing seemed to work. She wanted very much to assist her son, but did not know how to to go about doing it. She also stated that her current husband, who was a minister, had tried to assist Johnny on numerous occasions, but had given up because nothing seemed to work. She was told that Johnny's refusal to perform and behavioral difficulties arose from his perception of what happened between her and his father. She was told that Johnny felt that she was responsible for their separation, and that his nonachieving and deviant behavior was his way of getting back at her. She was encouraged to discuss the reasons for separation with Johnny, emphasizing why she felt it would be best for the two of them to leave his father. She was also advised to tell Johnny that he had the potential to achieve and that he would have to decide if he would achieve or not and that he would be responsible for the consequences of his behavior. She was also encouraged to communicate to him that he would be accepted and loved by her unconditionally, whether he achieved or not.

The change in Johnny was fairly slow; but school officials were tolerant, and worked closely with the home. He eventually resolved the hostilities he possessed toward his mother, reevaluated himself as an individual, and started to utilize his potential more effectively. He was promoted to tenth grade; and, when last observed, he was functioning quite adequately.

Case Report 6.7.

Suzy was a seven-year-old, second-grade student who was the older child in a family of two children. She was born out of wedlock and never knew her real father. Her mother later married and had a four-year-old boy from this relationship.

Suzy was referred to the school psychologist because her teacher felt that she was underachieving. Her Verbal, Performance, and Full Scale IQ scores derived from her performance on the WISC-R were found to be 109, 93, and 102, respectively. Suzy's emotional adjustment was satisfactory and her behavior was appropriate for her age.

An interview was arranged for the parents, but only the mother attended. It was apparent from the onset that the mother resented her daughter and that Suzy was aware of this disposition. The mother was encouraged to explore her feelings toward Suzy honestly, reflect on their past relationship, and try to determine if there had been shortcomings and resentments on either side. It was suggested that she should first try and identify difficulties; once they were discovered, she would try to resolve them. The mother was also made aware of the reasons for Suzy's refusal to achieve. It was suggested that Suzy's behavior (refusal to achieve) was her way of getting back at someone (her mother) who, she felt, had rejected her. The school officials agreed to monitor Suzy's behavior closely and to communicate with the mother daily in order to keep her informed of Suzy's progress. Suzy responded well to her mother's new way of behaving toward her, and benefited from the extra attention she received at school. Her achievement improved significantly; she successfully completed second grade; and, when last observed, she was working at grade level.

Case Report 6.8.

Harvie was a six-year-old, first-grade child who was the oldest child in a family of three children. He was the only boy and was three years older than his oldest sister. His mother was a homemaker and his father was a successful businessman who devoted most of his time to his business endeavors and left the rearing of the children to his wife.

Harvie was referred to the school psychologist by his teacher who felt that he was a depressed child who was regressing academically. Harvie's Verbal, Performance, and Full Scale IQ scores derived from his performance on the WISC-R were 124, 112, and 121, respectively.

The mother, after nearly an hour of discussion in a conference attended by both parents, stated that she found it difficult to show affection to her son. She, however, did not experience any difficulties showing affection to her daughters. The parents were informed that Harvie's behavior represented his way of dealing with the hostilities he possessed, because he felt that he had been removed from his position as center of the family and replaced by his younger sisters. The family was referred for counseling and encouraged to communicate to Harvie that he was loved as much as as the other children. The parents responded positively to the recommendations. They arranged to be seen for counseling and apparently communicated to Harvie that he was loved in the same fashion that his sisters were. Harvie reassessed his evaluation of himself; his self-esteem improved; and his academic achievement increased significantly.

The cases listed here, although all somewhat different, share some things in common. For instance, all of the children possessed average to superior intelligence, but failed to achieve at a level consistent with their ability. Underachievement in each case resulted from the child's inability to deal effectively with hostilities he/she possessed toward parents and the behavior in all cases was self-defeating and as a consequence the youngster stood to lose the most.

It is essential that teachers and educational psychologists note that children's hostilities are a consequence of their perceptions of how they feel their parents feel about them. The child's behavior is a consequence of the perceptions he possesses, and may or may not be congruent with reality as it actually exists. That is, the child's perceptions of how the parents feel may not be consistent with how the parents actually feel. The discrepancy however, is irrelevant, and has no affect on the child's behavior. If the child feels that his parents do not love him, he will respond in a fashion that reflects this disposition; and whether the parents love him or not, will have little, if any, effect on his behavior. It therefore becomes necessary to provide some form of intervention which will modify the child's perceptions of the relationships with his parents. The agent providing the intervention may vary from child to child, depending on the circumstances surrounding the individual case. In some cases, the intervention may be provided by parents, teachers, counselors, psychologists, by an agent in the community, or by several agents working together. Intervention, nevertheless, is essential, if the child is to resolve the conflict he is experiencing and reevaluate his perceptions of personal worth, which will, in turn, foster achievement.

Summary

Findings of research studies reviewed in the chapter indicate that there is a positive, significant relationship between reading and self-esteem. Research findings also indicate that reading disability is associated with emotional problems (Gates 1941; Knapp 1959; Dechant 1968) and personal maladjustment (Smith 1955; Knapp 1959; Spache 1957).

Remedial techniques implemented heretofore have often been ineffective in modifying reading disabilities frequently because the originators of these programs and techniques did not adequately build in mechanisms designed to facilitate the development of affective or emotional components which play intricate roles in the achievement process. Developers of these programs apparently did not realize that a reevaluation of perceptions of self-worth is essential in order for the child to modify his self-defeating (non-achieving) patterns, which will, in turn enable him to utilize his potential more effectively. Some form of intervention from external sources (e.g., teachers, parents, counselors) is needed in order to help the child to make this reassessment. Psychologists and educators, therefore, should direct more energies toward freeing the child from emotional conflicts which compel him to employ self-defeating patterns, which, in turn, impede academic achievement.

IV

ASSESSMENT OF SELF-ESTEEM

ENHANCING

7

MEASUREMENT OF THE SELF

In this chapter we will review a number of scales intended to measure self-regard. The following is a list of the most frequently used affective scales, designed to measure various aspects of self-regard.

Child Personality Scale. Amatora, Sr. M. (1957). The instrument is comprised of 22 traits which are measured on a ten-point scale. The rs of subjects who participated in the standardization of the scale ranged from .10 to .67. Fourteen of 22 rs were significant at the .01 level for 200 girls.

The Culture-Free Self-Esteem Inventory for Children, Forms A and B. Battle, J. (1981). Form A is comprised of 60 items and a total of five subscales, one which is a lie scale designed to measure defensiveness. Without the lie scale 50 items were intended to measure an individual's perception in four areas: self, peers, parents, and school. The items in the scale were selected from Coopersmith's (1967) *Self-Esteem Inventory*, Gough's (1965) *Adjective Checklist*, plus those developed by the author. The items are divided into two groups, those which indicate high self-esteem and those indicating low self-esteem. The individual checks each item either "yes" or "no," and the self-esteem score is the total number of items checked which indicate high self-esteem. Test-retest reliability for 198 boys and girls in grades three through six for 48 hours was .84 and .82 respectively. Test-retest reliability for 33 boys and girls over a two-year period was .74. Factor analysis and validity findings are presented in the manual.

Form B is comprised of 30 items and a total of five subscales, one of which is a lie scale designed to measure defensiveness. Without the lie scale 25 items were intended to measure an individual's perception in four areas: self, peers, parents, and school. The items in Form B are divided into two groups, those which indicate high self-esteem and those which indicate low self-esteem. The individual checks each item either "yes" or "no," and the self-esteem score is the total number of items checked which indicates high self-esteem. Test-retest reliability for 110 boys and girls enrolled in grades three through six for the total sample, boys, and girls, were .84, .80, and .87 respectively. Correlations between Forms A and B for 160 boys and girls in grades five and six were .89 and .80 respectively.

The Culture-Free Self-Esteem Inventory for Adults, Form AD. Battle, J (1981).
The scale is comprised of 40 items and a total of four subscales, including a lie scale designed to measure defensiveness. The other 32 items intended to measure an individual's self, personal, and social perception are divided into those indicating high self-esteem and those indicating low self-esteem. The individual checks each item "yes" or "no" and the self-esteem score is the total number of items checked which indicate high self-esteem. Test-retest correlations for a group of 127 males and females enrolled in an introductory educational psychology course were .81. The value for males was .79, for females .82. Factor analytic and validity findings are presented in the manual.

Questionaire for Self-Acceptance and Acceptance of Others. Berger, E. M. (1952).
An omnibus-type questionaire intended to measure self-acceptance of others. Matched-half reliability coefficients of 200 subjects who comprised the various subgroups participating in the standardization study were .746 or better. Construct validity was explored in terms of the correlation with three paragraphs written by 20 subjects and judged by four examiners on the basis of Scheerer's definition of self-accepting and other-accepting person. For self-acceptance, r was .897.

Bills' Index of Adjustment and Values. Bills, R. E. (1951-1954).
These scales utilize a (self-ideal) discrepancy score as well as a direct self-acceptance to index self-regard. One hundred twenty-four trait names were selected from Allport's list of 17,953 traits as representative, in the opinion of the test designer, of items which occur frequently in client-centered interviews. Forty-nine items showing greatest test-retest stability on pre-testing were retained in the final form. In regard to himself, subject gives three answers to each item: Column I: How often are you this sort of person? (Marked on a five-point scale from "most of the time" to "seldom.") Column II: How do you feel about being this way? (Marked on a five-point scale from "very much like" to "very much dislike.") Column III: How much of the time would you like this trait to be characteristic of you? (Marked on a five-point scale from "seldom" to "most of the time.") The sum of column I (with negative traits reversed) equals the self score. The sum of column II is taken as a measure of of self-acceptance. The sum of the discrepancies between columns I and II is taken as the (self-ideal) discrepancy, from which self-satisfaction is inferred. (The subject also answers these same questions about other people, defined in terms of a relevant peer group.) Split-half reliabilities for 100 college students ranged from .53 for self scores (column I) to .87 for (self-ideal) discrepancies (column I-column III). Six-week test-retest correlations, with varying numbers of subjects, ranged from .83 for self-acceptance (column II) to .90 for self (column I). Sixteen-week test-retest correlations, for varying numbers of subjects, ranged from .52 for (self-ideal) discrepancies (column I-column III), to .86 for self scores.

Self-Report Inventory. Bown, O. (1961).
The scale, which has English, Spanish, and French versions, is intended to measure one's phenomenological world. The present version is a 948-item scale with five-point answers from "like me" to "unlike me," contains eight, six-item scales. The alpha coefficient of 2,321 freshmen students for the six-item scale was .78. The value for the total scale was .87.

Stability of Self-Concept Scale. Brownfain, J. J. (1952).
This instrument is comprised of 25 items which the subject uses to rate himself four times to indicate: (1) his most favorable realistic self-concept ("positive self-concept"); (2) his most unfavorable

realistic self concept ("negative self-concept"); (3) his realistic, private self-concept; and (4) his most accurate estimate of himself as he believed other people in the group saw him ("social self-concept"). The "stability score" is obtained by subtracting "negative self-concept" on each of the 25 items and summing across all items without regard to sign.

Purdue Self-Concept Scale for Primary Grade Children. Cicirelli, V. G. (1977). The scale is intended to assess aspects of a child's self-concept involving his sense of social acceptance and competence in a number of areas.

Purdue Social Attitude Scale for Preschool Children. Cicirelli, V. G. (1977). The scale is intended to assess children's feelings and evaluations about persons, objects, and situations which represent peers, school, community, and home. The items are a series of cartoon picture stories. The examiner reads the captions and then asks the child to complete each story by choosing one of the three faces to express how he feels about the situation. The scales, which should be individually administered, are intended for use in research studies only and not for individual diagnosis of children.

Self-Esteem Inventory. Coopersmith, S. (1967). Form A has 58 items and a total of five subscales. One of the five subscales is a lie scale designed to measure defensiveness. The instrument, without the lie scale, has four subscales of 50 items concerned with perception in four areas: peers, parents, school, and self. The items in Coopersmith's scale were divided into two groups by agreement of five psychologists that they indicate either high or low self-esteem. The subjects check each item "like me" or "unlike me"; and the scores are reported as the total number correct on all scales, excluding the lie scale, which results in a maximum of 50 items. For convenience, the total self-esteem inventory score is multiplied by 2 so that the maximum score is 100. Test-retest reliability for 30 fifth-grade students over a five-week period was .88.

Form B consists of 25 items. The subject checks each item "like me" or "unlike me"; and the self-esteem score is reported as a single score with a maximum of 25. The number of correct responses is noted then multiplied by four (25 x 4 = 100), providing a figure which is comparable to the self-evaluation score obtained on Form A (excluding the lie scale).

Acceptance of Self and Acceptance of Others Questionaire. Fey, W. F. (1955, 1957, 1959). The split-half reliability coefficient for third-year medical students for acceptance of self equals .84. The value for freshmen medical students was .92.

Tennessee Self-Concept Scale. Fitts, W. (1964). This is a self-report scale intended to measure self-acceptance across many sub-areas. The scale is comprised of 90 items and five general categories: physical self, moral-ethical self, personal self, family self, and social self. Each of these areas is in turn divided into statements of self-identity, self-acceptance, and behavior. There are five response categories for each item, which range from (5) "completely true," to (1) "completely false." The total positive score for the 90 items yields the total score. Subscores can be computed for each of the five general categories. Test-retest reliability for 626 students, ages 12 through 68, over a two-week period, was .92. Test-retest correlations of scores earned on subscales for the same sample ranged from .70 to .90, with personally relevant constructs. Items retained in the final version of the scale correlated from .45 to .78 with the total score. The self-ideal discrepancy scores across four areas, for 63 subjects, correlated between .53 and .69 with each other.

Student Self-Rating Scale of Excellence (grades 13-16). Gadzella, B. M., and Fournet, G. P. (1976). This scale is designed to assess differences and changes during a semester in students' perceptions of themselves as quality students. The instrument consists of 37 student characteristics grouped into two categories: "in class," covering factors such as attendance, understanding of course objectives, note-taking and preparedness; and "out of class," including factors such as study habits and attitudes, student-student relationships, student-instructor relationships, and physical and emotional needs. The student rates himself on the characteristics several times during the semester.

Adjective Checklist. Gough, H. G., and Heilbrun, A. B., Jr. (1965). The scale consists of 300 adjectives, of which subjects check as many as they consider to be self-descriptive. The score is obtained by subtracting the number of adjectives which indicate low self-confidence from the total number marked. Test-retest coefficients for the self-confidence scale varied from .63 to .73 for periods of ten weeks to five and one-half years.

An Interpersonal Checklist Intended to Measure a Number of Variables Defined by the Interpersonal Personality System. LaForge, R., and Suczek, R. (1955). The checklist is used to measure (1) a self-description; (2) an ideal-self description; and (3) "self-acceptance" in terms of discrepancies between self and ideal-self descriptions.

Social Personality Inventory for College Women. Maslow, A. H. (1942). A self-report scale which is used to infer self-esteem. Test-retest correlations over a two-week period were .90. Eighty-one percent of the subjects were asked to estimate the accuracy of their own scores, and reported that they felt their score was fairly accurate or very accurate.

Miskimims Self-Goal Other Discrepancy Scale. Miskimims, R. W. (1971). The inventory is intended to measure self-concept from a clinical perspective. The scale, which requires that the subjects rate (1) themselves, (2) their goal for themselves, and (3) how family and friends see them on nine-point bipolar scales, contains four scales for each of three standard areas (general, social, and emotional).

The Primary Self-Concept Inventory. Muller, D. G., and Leonetti, R. (1974). This self-report scale is comprised of 20 items. Each item depicts at least one child in a positive role and at least one child in a negative role. The scale is designed to measure six aspects or factors of self-concept, which may be clustered into three major domains: the personal self (physical size; emotional state), the social-self (peer acceptance; helpfulness), and intellectual self (success, student-self). Test-retest reliability coefficients for samples of 372 and 100 subjects were .91 and .57, respectively.

Questionaire for Self-Acceptance and Acceptance of Others. Phillips, E. L. (1951). This is an omnibus-type questionaire which converts Scheerer's (1949) descriptions of the self and other-accepting person into simple statements. The questionaire is comprised of 50 statements, 25 concerning the self and 25 concerning others. A five-day test-retest correlation of the scores of college females yielded a correlation of .84 for self-items.

Piers-Harris Children's Self-Concept Scale. ("The way I feel about myself.") Piers, E. V. (1969). Eighty items taken from Jersild's (1952) collection of children's statements about what they liked and disliked about themselves. Items, which are answered "yes" or "no," comprise the following six categories: behavior, intellectual and school status, physical appearance and attributes, anxiety, popularity, and happiness and satisfaction. Test-retest reliability for periods of two and four months for 244 fifth-grade pupils yielded coefficients of .77.

Self-Esteem Scale. Rosenberg, M. (1965). The scale consists of ten items intended to measure the self-acceptance aspect of self-esteem. Response alternatives are scored on a four-point scale, which ranges from "strongly agree" to "strongly disagree," although they are scored only as agreement or disagreement. A Guttman scale reliability coefficient of .92 was obtained from the 3,024 high school juniors and seniors who comprised the standardization sample.

Personal Orientation Inventory. Shostrum, E. (1968). The scale is intended to measure self-actualization as defined by Maslow (1962). The inventory is comprised of 150 paired-choice items. The main measure of self-actualization involves inner-directedness and living in the present (time competence) but there are subscales for self-regard, self-acceptance, and other conceptions. There are no reported data on internal consistency. Test-retest correlations over one week for 48 college students were .84 and .71 for the major scales, and .75 and .80 for the self-regard and self-acceptance subscale.

Self-Perception Inventories. Soares, A., and Soares, L. (1965). This self-rating scale, which also has a peer rating form, uses six polar scales with four points. Subjects rate: (1) themselves, (2) how they think classmates see them, (3) how they think teachers see them, and (4) how they think parents see them. Subjects rate their ideal selves also. The bipolar scales consist of short sentences for young students and adjectives for older adolescents, adults, and student teachers. No data bearing on internal consistency are reported. Soares (personal communication) reports a preliminary test-retest reliability of .88 for self-ratings for an unspecified sample (Robinson and Shaver 1976, p. 104).

Self-Concept Inventory. Sherwood, J. J. (1962). The scale, which is based on self-ratings across several dimensions, contains a measure of realistic or aspired self-ratings to replace ideal-self ratings. It also contains "open" scales, which allow respondents to define their own dimensions for rating and an additional rating of the importance of each item to total self-concept. The revised scales are comprised of 15 bipolar dimensions with 11-point rating scales, plus three dimensions for which the end-points are defined by each respondent. Test-retest reliability for 57 psychology students over a two-week period was .82 for self-rating and .78 for importance.

Six-Point Scales for Friendliness, Likeability, Generosity, Intelligence, Sense of Humor. Wylie, R. C. (1957). Each point is defined by verbal description. Subjects rate themselves as they think members of a military peer group will rate them.

Social Self-Esteem Inventory. Ziller, R. et al. (1969). The scale consists of six circles arranged horizontally, followed by a list of people such as (1) doctor, (2) father, (3) friend, (4) a nurse, (5) yourself, or (6) someone you know who is unsuccessful. There are six such lists which all include "yourself." One is instructed to place each person in a circle. The farther to the left of the horizontal array one puts oneself, the higher one's social self-esteem. The form for children uses a vertical array of circles with the top indicating high esteem. No test-retest data are reported, but split-half reliability coefficients in the .80's have been reported.

Summary

Twenty-six scales intended to measure self-regard were reviewed in this chapter. All scales reviewed in this section have demonstrated the ability to assess various aspects of the self, but nevertheless are plagued by the major problem inherent in all self-report instruments, "the inability to effectively control for faking," in both positive and negative directions. The problem of "faking" is an acute one with children, because youngsters generally feel compelled to report favorable dispositions or those they feel the examiner expects. A number of test constructors (e.g., Coopersmith 1959; Battle 1981) have attempted to account for faking by building like items (those designed to measure defensiveness) into their scales. I have found these items to be effective in identifying youngsters who feel compelled to present themselves in a fashion which is not consistent with how they truly feel. Faking, nevertheless, continues to be a problem to which test developers must address themselves.

In spite of the problems associated with self-report inventories, I agree with the position taken by J. C. Nunnally: "Long ago the author came to the conclusion that generally the most valid, economical, sometimes the only way to learn about a person's sentiments is simply to ask him." Self-report inventories ask children how they feel about themselves, and in most instances children reveal how they truly feel.

8

ACTIVITIES THAT ENHANCE
SELF-ESTEEM AND ACHIEVEMENT

Self-esteem is one of the most important variables affecting the lives of all human beings. It is of particular importance to the developing child, because it determines to a great extent whether the child develops a mode of existence that is self-enhancing or one that is self-defeating. Questions often are asked by parents and teachers regarding the self-esteem of pupils are: (1) "Can teachers augment the self-esteem of their pupils?" and (2) "Why is it important for teachers to attend to the self-esteem needs of pupils?"

Can Teachers Augment the Self-Esteem of their Pupils?

Parents or parent surrogates are the most significant individuals determining the self-esteem of developing children. Once the child enters school teachers functions "in loco parentis," sharing many of the responsibilities of parents. Consequently they inherit the ability to affect children's perceptions of self-worth. The teacher is the most significant other affecting the self-esteem of children after they enter school. Support for this position is provided by W. D. Labenne and B. I. Green (1969), who stressed the important role that teachers play in the formation of children's perceptions of self-worth when they state:

> Any person who is intimately involved in the administration of rewards and punishments is in a position to become a significant other; it is not merely the ability or responsibility of administering the system. . . that makes a teacher a significant other. Rather it is the manner in which he uses his authority that causes him to have a potent impact (p. 27).

How teachers interact with their pupils significantly affects their students' self-esteem. For instance, J. W. Staines (1958) analyzed the responses and comments of a group of teachers and found that students with teachers who used democratic methods, who made positive comments, and who gave consideration to the child's self-concept, made positive changes in self-concepts of their children; whereas marked psychological insecurity and maladjustment were found in the children whose teachers emphasized correctness of subject matter. Teachers who emphasized correctness of subject matter did not recognize the important role that perceptions of self play in the educational process. Staines made the following comments in his discussion of the implications of his findings:

> The educational significance of the self is reaffirmed when it is realized that changes in the self picture are an inevitable part of both outcomes and conditions of learning in every classroom, whether or not the teacher is aware of them . . . . It is clear that teaching methods can be adapted so that definite changes of the sought will occur in the self. The self can be deliberately produced by suitable teaching methods (p. 109).

J. Canfield and H. C. Wells (1976) offer the following regarding teachers' ability to augment perceptions of self-worth:

> It is possible to change self-concepts, and it is possible for teachers to effect the changes—either way, positive or negative . . . . Many of us teach because we had a teacher or two who really had a significant impact on us. The impact was related to our self-concept. The teacher somehow communicated a sense of caring and a sense of our own personal worth. On the other hand, many of us have also experienced a teacher who humiliated us or our classmates through sarcasm and ridicule. These teachers make learning a negative experience. Teachers can and do affect pupils' self-concepts every day. You have a choice over what kind of effects you will have (p. 4).

Why is it Important for Teachers to Attend to the Self-Esteem Needs of Pupils?

It is important that teachers attend to the self-esteem of pupils, because self-esteem is an important variable affecting academic achievement. Research findings (e.g., Shaw et al. 1960; Battle 1978, 1979) clearly indicate that students who are experiencing academic difficulties at school percieve their worth as lower than do students who are apparently making satisfactory academic progress. Although teachers of school age children have traditionally emphasized the development of cognitive skills, they have generally tended to ignore the affective domain of the developing child. This neglect of the affective needs of developing children has contributed greatly to the many educational and societal problems we observe today, including underachievement and various forms of juvenile delinquency. Underachievement is a problem that is so widespread that in many instances underachievers represent the majority of the pupils in the student population. Estimates of the number of underachievers in our schools differ, but researchers generally agree that the percentage is high. For instance, H. M. Alter (1952) found 43 percent of the student population of a suburban junior-senior high school to be underachievers. Other theorists (e.g., Wedemeyer 1953; Ritter and Thorn 1954) state that between 20 and 50 percent of students work below their potential and as a consequence may be classified as underachievers. Underachievers are well represented in juvenile delinquent populations. For instance, L. T. Yeudall (1977) studied incarcerated juvenile delinquents and found that 78 percent of them were underachievers experiencing severe learning deficiencies. Because self-esteem and achievement are so closely interrelated, it is essential that educators develop procedures designed to enhance self-esteem. C. Lipton (1963) offers the following regarding the relationship between self-esteem and achievement:

> The roots of desire to learn are deep and multifaceted. The development of a self-worth and self-value is one of the most important and significant of these branches. To know oneself and to value oneself contributes mightily to the development of an able learner, a curious learner, and a mature learner (p. 211).

Only recently have psychologists, educators, and parents realized the important role that self-esteem plays in the educational process. Nowadays, there is a high level of interest in the phenomenon of self-esteem. This realization (regarding the importance of self-perceptions in the achievement process) has resulted in the current emphasis on affective-domain training in our schools. It has also resulted in an increasing number of requests from teachers and parents for seminars and workshops dealing with the issue of self-esteem. Parents and teachers are particularly interested in learning means or ways of enhancing self-esteem in children. Unfortunately, empirical data describing specific means of enhancing self-esteem have not been hitherto convincingly discerned.

We assume that self-esteem is an antecedent of achievement, and that the concept of self-worth is a learned structure which develops as the child interacts with significant others. Support for this belief is provided by Staines (1958), who stated:

> The concept of self tends to be a learned structure which grows mainly from the comments made by other people and from inferences drawn by children out of their experiences in home, school, and other social groups.

Staines assumed that significant others could alter the self-concepts of the children with whom they interacted. Other theorists (e.g., Davidson and Lang 1960; Rosen, Levinger, and Lippitt 1960; Videbeck 1960; and Brookover and Gottlieb 1964) have demonstrated that others can modify the self-concepts of children. S. Rosen, C. Levinger, and R. Lippitt (1960), in their investigation of the role of group-relevant determinants, demonstrated that individuals who are significant to another person, can significantly influence that person's concept of self. These investigators found a positive, significant relationship between an individual's desire for change and the wishes of others. Similar findings were reported by W. E. Clarke (1960) in his study of the relationship between academic performance in college students and their expected performance. Clarke found a significant, positive relationship between a student's academic performance and his perception of academic expectancies held for him by significant others. R. Videbeck (1960) also reported data which support the proposition that "self-conceptions are learned and that the evaluative reactions of others play a significant part in the learning process." In a study designed to determine the effects of evaluation by external sources, Videbeck demonstrated that significant changes in self-ratings could occur after one critique by an evaluator.

Brookover and Gottlieb, in their text entitled *A Sociology of Education*, summarize their views of the role that the expectations of others play in conceptions of self in the following passage:

> In this context, the self is the intervening variable between normative patterns of the social group or the role expectations held by significant others on the one hand, and the learning of the individual on the other. We hypothesize that, for the expectations of others to be functional in a particular individual's behavior, they must be internalized and become a part of the person's conception of him-

self. Although we recognize the relevance of self in all aspects of human behavior, our interest at this point is in a particular aspect of self as it functions in the school learning situation.

We postulate that the child acquires, by taking the role of the other, a perception of his own ability as a learner of the various types of skills and subjects which constitute the school curriculum. If the child perceives that he is unable to learn mathematics or some other area of behavior, this self-concept of his ability becomes the functionally limiting factor of his school achievement. *Functional limit* is the term used to emphasize that we are speaking not of genetic organic limits on learning, but rather of those perceptions of what is appropriate, desirable, and possible for the individual to learn. We postulate the latter as the limits that actually operate within broader organic limits in determining the nature or extent of the particular behavior learned (p. 469).

If self-esteem is an antecedent of achievement, and if the two variables are closely associated and interrelated, it seems that educators should develop and implement programs which will enhance self-esteem and in turn, foster achievement. In the remaining chapter, we provide summaries of projects and programs which have proven to be effective in enhancing the self-esteem of participating subjects.

Although the procedures which follow have proven to be effective means of enhancing self-esteem, one may find that a given procedure or interventive measure may induce significant shifts in some areas of self-esteem, but not in all areas. For instance, I consult with 15 principals in a large metropolitan school system in North Western Alberta who are attempting to enhance the self-esteem of their entire student populations. The strategies adopted by these educators vary greatly, and range from providing experiences such as those incorporated in the DUSO and *Magic Circle* programs, to using psychodrama and videotape presentations. Preliminary results indicate that the procedures implemented by the principals generally induce significant shifts in the social self-esteem of participating pupils. The principals have informed me that they are pleased with the results because their major intentions were to enhance social self-esteem. They feel that enhanced social self-esteem of pupils will facilitate the development of more positive interpersonal interactions between pupils and between pupils and teachers. Facilitating the development of more positive interpersonal interactions in schools is a highly desirable objective to pursue because, if more positive interpersonal relations can be established, there will be fewer behavior management problems in the school environment.

Activity A

Brookover, W. B., Paterson, A., and Sailor, T.

Brookover, Paterson, and Sailor (1965), in their study of the relationship of self-images to achievement in junior high school subjects, demonstrated means of modifying the self-concepts of ability of low-achieving students.

The investigators assumed that they could enhance the self-concept of ability of low-achieving students, and subsequently, increase their achievement through:

1. Modification of images and expectations held by significant others (parents in this case).
2. Direct contact with an "expert" who would communicate information to enhance self-concept of ability.

3. Interaction with a counselor, holding positive and high expectations for the students.

The specific hypothesis tested in the study were:

1. Systematically developed increases in perceived evaluation and expectations which parents (as significant others) hold of low-achieving students will result in parallel changes in these students' self-concepts of ability.
2. Systematically developed increases in self-concepts of ability (as induced under hypothesis number 1) will result in increases in the students' level of school achievement.
3. The self-concepts of low-achieving students can be enhanced by having a person who is presented as an expert give these students evidence that they are more able than they perceive themselves to be.
4. Increases in self-concept of ability (as induced by hypothesis number 3) will result in increases in the level of school achievement.
5. The self-concepts of low-achieving students can be enhanced by a counselor who systematically provides a set of high evaluations.
6. The increases in self-concept of ability (as induced by hypothesis number 5) will result in increases in level of school achievement.

The investigators also examined the four following theoretically derived hypotheses:

1. The students' perception of the evaluations of academic ability held by significant others is associated with their self-concept of ability at each grade level.
2. Changes over time in the perceived evaluations of significant others are associated with changes over time in self-concept of ability.
3. The students' self-concept of ability is associated with their academic achievement at each grade level.
4. Changes over time in self-concept of academic ability are associated with changes over time in academic achievement.

The investigators tested three experimental designs in their attempts to modify the self-concepts of ability of their subjects.

Experiment A (parental experiment). This experiment was designed to study the effects of working with parents in order to influence children. The experiment was designed especially to determine if changes in expectations which parents hold of their children would result in changes in the self-concept of ability of the child, and to determine if such changes are manifested in changes in academic achievement. The selected group of parents who participated in this experiment met weekly for a one-year period and participated in group discussions in which various topics relating to self-perceptions and achievement were discussed. The purpose of meeting with the parents was to enable them:

1. To help the child to acquire and enhance self-concept of academic ability.
2. To develop in the parent a recognition that his child's academic weaknesses could be improved.
3. To effect a greater parental feeling of confidence and responsibility for maximum student achievement (p. 77).

Experiment B (expert experiment). This experiment was designed to study the effects of formal presentations by a person defined as an "expert" on low-achieving students. The expert met with selected groups of students and assured them that they could do better academically. He also communicated information intended to enhance self-concept of ability.

Experiment C (counselor experiment). This experiment represented an investigation of the effects of counseling on low-achieving students. The experiment was designed specifically to determine whether the self-concept of low-achieving students who perceive that their parents hold low expectations of them could be raised by a counselor who could provide a set of high expectations and whether such changes are reflected in achievement. The counselor interacted with a selected group of subjects and exhibited positive and high expectations for the students.

The primary idea communicated in each experimental group stressed that the limits of ability, though affected by innate and other factors, are rarely attained in one's performance. Subjects were also told that there are other important factors which influence one's performance—for example, such factors as how one feels about a subject, interest in it, or whether one defines a subject as an appropriate area for good achievement. The idea of the importance of achievement was also stressed in each group (p. 39).

The investigators presented the following four goals of treatment:

1. A more positive self-concept and an acceptance of one's abilities on the part of the low-achieving students.
2. A recognition of academic weaknesses, but also a recognition that weaknesses are not fixed and that they can be overcome.
3. A feeling of responsibility in attaining higher achievement.
4. An improvement of school achievement as manifested in academic grades (p. 38).

Findings from three, one-year experiments with ninth-grade students and a longitudinal study of approximately 500 students in an urban school system revealed that a significant increase in both self-concept of ability and grade-point average was effected by working with parents who represented academic significance to their children. "Expert" and counseling treatments, however, failed to induce significant changes in either self-concept or achievement.

Brookover, Paterson, and Sailor concluded the following from their longitudinal investigation:

1. Self-concept of ability is a significant factor in achievement at all levels, seventh through tenth grades.
2. The perceived evaluations of significant others are a major factor in self-concept of academic ability at each grade level, eight through ten.
3. Change or stability in the perceived evaluations of others is associated with change or stability in self-concept.
4. Change or stability in self-concept of ability is associated with change or stability in achievement. The associated change in achievement is noted, however, only over longer periods of time (three years).
5. Change or stability of perceived evaluations of others is not likely to be associated with change or stability in academic achievement.
6. The relationship of self-concept to achievement is not associated with school attended.
7. Socioeconomic class has a low relationship to self-concept of ability and achievement. Furthermore, the relationship between socioeconomic status to achievement decreases from grade seven through ten. Change analysis

indicated no association between socioeconomic status and self-concept or achievement.

8. Self-concept is not merely a reflection of memory of past performance.
9. Self-concept of ability in specific subjects is less stable in its relationship with total achievement than is general self-concept of ability.
10. There are no consistent sex differences in the relationship of self-concept with achievement.
11. The only consistent sex difference was that female responses showed a greater relationship between perceived parental and teacher evaluations and self-concept of ability than was the case for males.
12. Self-concept of ability is not merely a reflection of memory of how teachers graded in the past; but memory of how teachers graded is more relevant than memory of past performance.
13. Self-concept is not merely a reflection of past achievement.
14. Changes between the associations of one major variable with another over the longitudinal period are not accounted for by group changes in responses to the measures of these variables at any grade level (e.g., changes in grading standards). The student body tended to show the same distribution on each of the major variables at all grade levels (pp. 201-202).

Commentary

Findings from this extensive, well designed longitudinal study indicates that concepts of ability, which are associated with academic achievement, are derived primarily from perceived evaluations of significant others. Parents, therefore, are an effective resource which teachers, counselors, and educational psychologists may use to enhance the self-concept of ability of participating students, which will, in turn, foster academic achievement. Additional support for this theoretical orientation is provided by evidence from numerous research studies which indicate that a student's performance in task orientated situations is influenced directly by his self-concept. A leading spokesman for this position, R. M. Roth (1959), while investigating the role of self-concept in achievement concluded, "In terms of the conception of self, individuals have a definite investment to perform as they do. With all things being equal, those who do not achieve choose not to do so, while those who do achieve, choose to do so."

Activity B

Aronson, E., with Blaney, N., Sikes, J., Stephan, C., and Snapp, M. (1975).

Aronson and colleagues developed an instructional technique which they called the "Jigsaw Teaching Method" that they felt would promote cooperation and enhance the self-esteem of participating students. The investigators argued that we should deemphasize competitiveness in our classrooms and encourage our children to learn to use one another as resources, rather than competitors; we should encourage cooperation and mutual respect, rather than competitiveness and opposition. To test this theoretical assumption and determine the effectiveness of their jigsaw-puzzle method, they conducted a small pilot study in which they divided a fifth-grade class into small learning groups of five or six students each, and set it up so that competitiveness would be incompatible with success. The children would have to cooperate with each other in order to succeed. To do this, they eliminated the teacher as a major source of knowledge, and structured the class so that children would have to treat each other as resources. The intervention to which the children were exposed, involved the introduction of the jigsaw-puzzle method, in which each child would have a piece of the information which was vital for the completion of the assignment. All members would have to work together and rely on one another in order to complete the task successfully. The slowest member of the group, thus, was as essential as the brightest member. No one individual could experience success without the aid of everyone in the group. Competition, therefore, would be reduced and cooperation would be fostered. It soon became clear to the children that each member had a unique, essential contribution to make.

The pilot study exposed the jigsaw-puzzle technique to the children one hour per week for a two-week period. The class was divided into two equal groups; one-half participating in the jigsaw technique, and the other half learning the traditional way. Approximately one-half of the students in the control group receiving traditional instruction, worked in small, competitive groups with a graduate student who served as teacher. The other controls worked with the classroom teacher. At the end of the two-week period, the investigators measured the extent of the youngsters' liking for one another, and found that the children's liking for one another increased significantly for the experimental group; whereas there was no significant change in liking among children in the control groups. Only the children in the jigsaw-puzzle group increased their liking for their team members.

The investigators, encouraged by the results of their pilot study, extended the project the following year and included ten classrooms of students in various sections of the city of Austin, Texas.

The experimental classes were comprised of 177 Anglos, 76 Blacks, 41 Chicanos, and one Oriental; the control classes were comprised of 50 Anglos, 9 Blacks, 20 Chicanos, and two Orientals. The study, which lasted for six consecutive weeks, was designed to determine: (1) how much the children would come to like each other; (2) how much they liked school, this year and last; (3) how they felt about themselves; and (4) how well they did in school. The data collected from the study revealed the following:

1. Children in the jigsaw groups liked their peers more at the end of the six weeks than children in the traditional classrooms. This was particularly true for Anglos and Blacks.

2. Students in the jigsaw groups saw each other as learning resources; those in the traditional classroom did not.

3. Overall, children in the experimental group showed more positive attitudes toward school over the six-week period, while the children in the traditional classes became progressively more negative toward school. Among the Blacks, however, attitudes toward school worsened in both groups—slightly in the jigsaw-puzzle groups, and enormously in the traditional classes. The jigsaw technique, while it did not make Black children love school, at least arrested the rapid growth of their dislike for school that happened in regular classes.

4. Children in the jigsaw groups had stronger and more positive self-concepts at the end of the experiment; their self-esteem improved, and they felt increasingly more important in school, than did children in the traditional classrooms. Generally, all the children felt better about themselves when they were not in school (they felt more important on Saturdays than on school days); but this discrepancy was much smaller in the jigsaw group. This was

especially true for Black children in the experimental group; their feelings of importance in school were only slightly lower than such feelings on weekends.

5. The data on performance are stronger than they were in the pilot study. The students in the cooperative groups showed a significant improvement in grades during the course of the study, while the students in the control condition actually showed a decrease (p. 49).

Commentary

The investigators demonstrated that the jigsaw-puzzle method was effective in promoting happiness among children, and showed that youngsters felt better about themselves, liked their classmates better, and that these positive results did not interfere with learning and performance. Results obtained from classrooms throughout the city of Austin, Texas, indicated that the jigsaw-puzzle method was in no way inferior to the traditional methods of instruction in terms of learning and performance; but it was superior in terms of fostering group affection and friendship.

Activity C

Beker, J.

Beker (1960), in his study of the effects of school camping on the self-concepts and social relationship of participants, hypothesized that:

1. Social and emotional growth can be facilitated or stimulated in a social climate that makes it possible for children to exert initiative and self-determination within a context of social awareness and clear limits, and with the assistance of sensitive, understanding, but non-constricting adult guidance and leadership.

2. School camping, from the very nature of the situation, tends to provide this kind of social climate.

Beker studied 261 subjects from 13 sixth-grade classes in the Long Island, New York Public Schools, who participated in a total of seven school encampments. A comparable group of 96 controls who were pre- and post-tested only. A self-concept scale and a social-distance scale were administered to all subjects at school on three occasions. The first administration occurred one day prior to leaving for camp; the second ten days later (the next day after returning from camp); and the final one between ten weeks and three months after the encampments terminated. The author subsequently:

1. Compared the responses made by each subject on each item during the three administrations of the self-concept list and social-distance scale. A changed response by a subject on any item was recorded as positive or negative.

2. Applied the statistics of binomial probability to the data to determine the statistical significance of the proportion of positive shifts to negative shifts noted on each item. It was thus possible to compare the camper group with the control group on the basis of the number of self-concept items and social-distance scale items that showed statistically significant positive or negative shifts from the first administration to the second and from the first to

the third.

Findings concerning the self-concept are presented in Table 8.1.

TABLE 8.1. *Number of Items Showing Significant Shifts on the Self-Concept Checklist.*

		Number of Items Showing Significant Shifts			
Shifts	*N*	Boys	Girls	Combined	N Items Showing No Sig. Shift
First to Second Administration:					
Experimental	261	15+	11+	22+	23
Control	96	3+	3+	4+, 1−	42
Reliability (*p*)		.01	.05	.001	.001
First to Third Administration:					
Experimental	261	22+	19+	35+	11
Control	96	6+	4+	8+	36
Reliability (*p*)		.001	.001	.001	.001
	357				

Note 1: The difference from the second to the third administration shown by the experimental group was reliable at the .01 level for the number of items showing significant shifts by the entire group and for the number showing no significant shift. It was not reliable at the .05 level for either sex alone in the experimental group, or for any of the four categories in the control group.

Note 2: The checklist consisted of 47 items. The rows total more than 47 because some items shifted in more than one of the three categories listed.

Source: Beker, J. 1960. The influence of school camping on the self-concepts and social relationships of sixth-grade school children. *Journal of Educational Psychology* 51:352-356. Reprinted by permission of the author.

The data presented in Table 8.1 indicate that the change noted on the second administration of the self-concept checklist, immediately after the experimental (camp) period, markedly favored the campers over the control group. There were significant positive shifts on many more items by campers of both sexes than by controls. The data presented in Table 8.1, furthermore, indicate that, although an increased number of items showing significant positive shifts appeared for both groups on third administration, the difference between the groups was even greater and in the same direction. That is, it was found that the experimental group (campers) showed significantly more positive shifts on many more items than the control group.

The five self-concept items on which the experimental group showed the greatest positive change relative to the change shown by the control group in the second and third administration were: (1) I am a dependable person, (2) I have trouble making up my mind, (3) I get upset too easily, (4) I worry about what others think of me, and (5) I have some outstanding abilities.

Findings concering social relationships are presented in Table 8.2.

TABLE 8.2. *Shifts in Self Social Distance Scores.*

Shifts	First to Second Administration		First to Third Administration	
	Experimental (N =247)	Control (N = 85)	Experimental (N = 247)	Control (N = 85)
Total	219	76	232	77
Positive	.68	.61	.61	.52
Significance (p)	.05	ns	.05	ns

Note: The differences between the proportions of the experimental and control groups were not reliable on either the second or the third administrations.

Source: Beker, J. 1960. The influence of school camping on the self-concepts and social relationships of sixth-grade school children. *Journal of Educational Psychology* 51:352-356. Reprinted by permission of the author.

The data presented in Table 8.2 indicate that the self social-distance scores of the two groups were not significantly different. The results, however, did indicate that school camping had some positive influence on campers' self social-distance scores.

Commentary

Beker presents convincing evidence which indicates quite strongly that the camping experience can be effective in promoting the development of positive self-concepts in participating youngsters. Results obtained by Beker also indicate that the effects of the camping experience was not a transient one, but was evident in even greater magnitude after a lapse of more than ten weeks. It appears that school camping can have a markedly positive impact on children's self-concepts. Results, presented by Beker, also indicate that camping, though it may improve social relationships among participating children, however, does not appear to significantly affect these relationships.

Activity D

Youth-Tutoring-Youth Programs.

The use of student tutors is a technique which has been used by many teachers for centuries. Teachers have, for example, traditionally employed high-achieving students to assist their low-achieving classmates. The use of student-tutors in a systematic fashion, however, is a fairly recent occurrence. Teachers, moreover, have basically been concerned with enhancing the achievement levels of the student receiving the tutorial instruction; they have generally not concerned themselves with the effects the tutorial process had on tutors. Recent findings, however, indicate that tutors usually benefit as much from the tutorial proces as tutees (Frager and Stern 1970); Allen and Feldman 1972); and in some instances tutors benefit *more* than tutees. Support for the latter position is provided by R. D. Cloward (1972), who found that tenth and eleventh-grade students who tutored younger children for a seven-month period, showed a significantly greater increase in reading achievement scores than a comparable control group who did not function as tutors. Cloward also found that the gains made by tutors in reading were greater than those experienced by their tutees in reading.

An abundant amount of research findings indicate that the tutor may benefit in numerous ways from his involvement in the teaching process. For instance, observers of tutorial programs have reported that tutors' motivation, sense of responsiblity, self-esteem, and attitudes toward school have shown a positive shift. Consequently, many schools, encouraged by the prospects of positive effects which usually occur when older children teach younger children, have initiated and implemented some form of tutoring program (Gartner, Kohler, and Reissman 1971).

Realization of the positive effects that children usually experience when participating in tutorial programs has motivated the National Commission on Resources for Youth to encourage the development and implementation of Youth-Tutoring-Youth programs throughout the United States. The first Youth-Tutoring-Youth program sponsored by the National Commission on Resources for Youth was piloted in Newark and Philadelphia in the summer of 1967. This project employed 200 tutors, age 14 and 15, who were enrolled in the Neighborhood Youth Corps to teach reading to 400 younger children on a one-to-one basis, four days per week, for a seven-week period. All tutors were low-achieving youngsters who were two years behind academically and/or were experiencing behavior problems in their schools. Findings from this initial study indicated that participating youngsters who functioned as tutors experienced significant gains in reading. It was also noted that the rate of absenteeism on the part of the tutors was basically nonexistent, and interest was maintained at a high level throughout the project. For instance, only seven of the original 200 tutors left the program; and those who left, did so because of illness or in order to obtain a higher paying job. Teachers reported a radical, positive change in attitudes of tutors in regard to their achievement and willingness to assume responsibility; and parents reported a "growing confidence" and a "pride in their child's role as teacher."

The findings of the pilot study motivated the National Commission on Resources for Youth to encourage widespread adaptation of in-school and after-school Youth-Tutoring-Youth programs. The commission began a series of workshops throughout the United States to create interest in tutorial programs and to train individuals to operate these programs. This impetus greatly increased the interest in tutorial programs throughout the United States, and in 1973 there were over 500 cities that had youth-tutoring programs. The commission, in addition to establishing Youth-Tutoring-Youth programs in schools, was also able to to link tutoring with the Teacher Corps, VISTA, Title I ESEA programs, and the Career Opportunities Programs of the United States Office of Education.

Research findings indicate that one-to-one tutoring produces a number of advantages including:

1. It is very economical. A teacher who has 12 children in any specialized group or class (learning disabled, mentally retarded, educationally disabled, etc.) could tutor each of those children on a one-to-one basis for 30 minutes each per day. Since some will need fewer than five sessions per week, the tutor can work with, say, 15 or more children per week individually. She will move those 15 children along at least three times the rate that she could teach them in a class as one group. In a two-year time segment, therefore, she will significantly help at least 45 children (3 x 15) instead of 12. In terms of educational productivity and efficiency she does not need mountains of specialized audio-visual equipment and other expensive materials—nor a classroom—with which to operate. So money is saved there, too.

2. Tutoring neither pigeonholes children nor deprives them of other special services as do special classes for learning disabled, mentally retarded or educationally disabled children. The MR or LD or ED child goes to his tutor for individual "meditation." He remains unlabled to his peers. With tutoring he is not deprived of individual help as he is when in a specialized class. Thus, the child with learning disabilities can also receive tutoring for his specific deficits; and children with "multiple problems" can receive help across the board from their tutors.

3. Tutoring allows for individualized prescriptions and programming for individual children. Obviously, the special class teacher almost always tends to teach the entire class or segments of it. Almost all referred children are so unique in their patterns of disabilities, handicaps, and deficits (and strengths), that they cannot be satisfactorily grouped for class teaching as is popularly supposed. Only tutoring can effectively insure individualized programs and prescriptions, quickly and satisfactorily carried through to completion. They can be "tailor-made."

4. Tutoring allows for the motivation of the child from many sources. Motivation is 70 to 80 percent of anyone's success story—and that applies to all children. When a child is individually tutored along with regular class placement, everyone has high motivating standards for him—including the child himself. His teacher wants him to be at grade level; his tutor wants him to be at grade level; his parents want him to be at grade level; and the child himself, in among the pressures of the peer group, wants to be at grade level. Additionally, the tutor and the classroom teacher can prescribe and implement personalized, positive, behavior-motivating programs for him which will also spur him on.

5. Tutoring does not harm a child socially, as may special class or school placement. This is obvious, provided children are not labeled by the teachers and other school personnel. It can become a privilege and honor to be tutored, especially if gifted children are included in the tutoring system so their talents can be fully developed.

6. Tutoring saves years of a child's life in terms of enrichment and gathering and pleasurable achievement. Most important of all, tutoring enables the child to benefit from regular schooling much earlier and more quickly than any specialized class placement technique. Who should deprive a child from

learning to read and enjoy learning three times more quickly through tutoring than he would have in a special class? This last reason for tutoring is undeniable because it is the very heart of what education is all about.

The interest in student-tutoring projects has grown rapidly over the past several years; and many programs, including the ones summarized in the following activity, have proven to be effective in enhancing self-esteem as well as academic achievement.

Activity E

Mettee, D. R., Williams, A., and Reed, H. D. (1972).

These investigators conducted a project designed to facilitate enhancement of self-image and improve reading performance of young Black ghetto males who exhibited: (1) poor reading performance and habitual academic underachievement in general; (2) low self-esteem (negative self-image) both generally and in terms of academics; (3) a clear tendency not to benefit from the specific successes provided by remedial programs (as well as generally reacting unfavorably toward such rehabilitative efforts [e.g., retaining their negative self-images and continuing to read poorly]).

The investigators employed 58 control subjects ages seven to ten, and a comparable group of 58 experienced subjects who received one-to-one tutorial instruction in reading, provided by Black and Anglo university undergraduate students, once a week in two-hour sessions, for a five-month period. The 58 experimental subjects were also exposed to three forms of self-image enhancement procedures, which constituted a variable with the following three levels: (1) relevant positive feedback or indirect enhancement only; (2) direct image enhancement, plus relevant positive feedback without change-supports; and (3) direct image enhancement, plus relevant positive feedback with three change-supports. Each tutorial session consisted of two 45-minute reading periods and a 30-minute image-enhancement phase. In the relevant positive feedback or indirect-enhancement-only condition, positive feedback was provided by tutors; but there was no direct communication containing persuasive content designed to upgrade what the student thought about himself in general or his academic competency in particular. The direct-image-enhancement-plus-relevant-positive-feedback with no-change-support sessions were led by a Black male graduate student with a ghetto background, designated the "image-builder," and included all students and tutors present that day. These sessions consisted of examining the existing attitudes each student possessed concering himself and his race and identifying the bases and origins of these self-feelings. The subjects and tutors also explored negative stereotypes held by society toward Blackness and examined Black history and Black culture, which revealed the irrational and invalid bases of negative stereotypes. The direct-image-enhancement-plus-relevant-positive-feedback-with-three-change-supports conditions added additional provisions to the image sessions, which were intended to implement the change-supports. The major operational differences between the change-supports and no-change-supports conditions was that change-support tutors were trained to assist the image-builder in the image-enhancing sessions; whereas tutors were not trained in the no-support conditions. The training of the change-support tutors involved informing tutors of the specific psychological supports on a one-to-one basis with their tutees. Tutors in the change-support conditions were also trained to participate in the image-enhancement sessions and to support the image builder's arguments with active displays of group consensus.

The investigators found that the data collected one month and one year following the program revealed that direct image enhancement, if accompanied by change-sup-ports, induced significant long-term, persuasive, positive change in self-image, both with respect to student self-feelings and student behavior. Reading performance did not show significant change one month after the program concluded, but significant gains in reading scores were observed one year later for students with enhanced self-images who had male tutors.

Commentary

The investigators convincingly demonstrated that young children can, with exter-nal assistance and support can enhance their images of self, in spite of strong conditioning and indoctrination by parents and significant others in the home environment. A practical implication which may be derived from the findings is that sources beyond the immediate home environment (e.g., schools, churches, civic groups) can be used as effective instru-ments for enhancing the self-perceptions of young children.

Activity F

Special Class Placement.

Psychologists and educators generally agree that special class placement affects the self-esteem of children. These authorities, however, have assumed two widely diver-gent positions. Some assume that special class placement has a negative effect, whereas others insist the effect is enhancing. Opponents of special class placement for children experiencing learning difficulties typically argue that isolation and segregation of these children tend to foster negative feelings of self-worth. Proponents of special class place-ment, on the other hand, argue that the environment of the special class, which generally is less competitive, tends to reduce the anxieties and frustrations of children experiencing learning problems and therefore, as a consequence, tends to foster the development of positive feelings of self-worth (Battle 1979).

I studied 150 boys and girls, ages seven through fourteen, enrolled in regular and special education classes, and found that special class placement significantly enhanced the self-esteem and perceptions of ability of children experiencing learning problems. Findings of the study are summarized in Table 8.3.

Data presented in Table 8.3 indicate that children who were placed in special classes experienced significant gains in self-esteem and perception of ability over a one-year period, whereas subjects in regular classes (those making satisfactory progress) did not.

In another study, J. Andriashek and I (1980) studied learning-disabled children, ages eight to twelve, who had been placed in special education programs because they were experiencing academic deficits of two years or more in reading and arithmetic. Par-ticipating students were ramdomly assigned to two groups: (1) those who were integrated in regular classes for a portion of the school day (experimental group), and (2) those who remained in self-contained special education classes for the entire school day (control group). Experimental subjects were integrated in regular classes for science, music, health, and physical education, but received instruction in reading, and arithmetic in their self-contained special education classrooms. Findings of the study are presented in Table 8.4.

Data displayed in Table 8.4 indicate that special education subjects who were partially integrated, experienced significantly higher gains in self-esteem than those who

TABLE 8.3. *Means and Standard Deviations on Self-Esteem and Perception-of-Ability Scores for Regular and Special Education Students.*

Group	N	Pretest (June 1977)		Posttest (June 1978)	
		Mean	S.D.	Mean	S.D.
			Self-Esteem		
Regular	75	36.78	8.42	38.04	9.08
Special	68	31.35	8.18	35.60	7.80
			Perception of Ability		
Regular	83	48.22	11.00	47.88	11.81
Special	68	37.27	11.02	43.60	11.66

TABLE 8.4. *Pre- and Posttest Means for Experimental and Control Groups.*

Subscale	Experimental		Control	
	Pretest Mean	Posttest Mean	Pretest Mean	Posttest Mean
Total	31.5	33.7	37.1	33.5
General	13.0	14.1	14.9	13.7
Social	4.1	4.4	6.2	5.9
School	6.8	7.2	7.3	6.4
Parents	7.6	7.6	9.0	7.9

were not partially integrated. Findings indicate that mainstreaming of special education students for part of the school day is an effective way of bolstering the self-esteem of children with learning problems. This significant shift in perception of self-worth by subjects who were mainstreamed probably occurred because the children who were integrated for part of the school day viewed this experience positively. Thus, they considered it to be a success experience. The experience of coping successfully with the requirements of both special and regular classes significantly enhanced perceptions of self-worth.

D. M. Smith's research group (1977) studied 206 children enrolled in 23 self-contained classes for children with learning disabilities, and found that special class placement did not have a negative effect on the self-concepts of participating students. In another investigation these same theorists studied the effects of partial mainstreaming on the self-concepts of learning disabled children enrolled in self-contained special classes. In this study, a group of learning-disabled children were randomly selected and placed in a program which consisted of half-day integration in regular classrooms during reading and math periods. A comparable group of learning-disabled children remained in self-contained classrooms for the entire school day, and functioned as controls. Subjects were tested on three occasions. The first occurred at the beginning of the school year before the children were mainstreamed. The second test administration occurred one month later; and the final administration occurred near the end of the school year, during May. Findings of the study are summarized in Table 8.5.

TABLE 8.5. *Means of Self-Concept Scores of Participating Subjects.*

| | Self-Concept | | |
Group	Test 1 Mean	Test 2 Mean	Test 3 Mean
Comparison (not mainstreamed)	53.08	55.32	55.20
Experimental (mainstreamed)	52.60	58.92	63.68

Data presented in Table 8.5 indicate that partial mainstreaming significantly augmented the self-esteem of participating students; whereas children remaining in self-contained classrooms for the entire day showed a small initial increase and then a leveling off of their self-concepts.

Although results derived from findings in these studies are positive and encouraging, special class placement is not necessarily the best solution for children experiencing learning problems. It, however, is better to place these children in special classes than to have them remain in regular classes with their problems. A better solution would be to develop specific remedial and instructional strategies which would enable these children to utilize their potential more effectively and experience greater degrees of academic success.

Summary

The programs and procedures presented in this chapter by no means represent a complete or comprehensive list of the available means of enhancing self-esteem. Other procedures have proven to be effective in successfully enhancing the self-esteem of children. For instance, L. Carlton and R. H. Moore (1968) found that a program of self-directive dramatization which enabled children at different levels of ability to select materials and interact with one another was effective in significantly enhancing the children's self-concepts and reading ability levels.

Kokovich (1970) employed mentally able sixth-grade pupils to tutor grade-one students who were poor readers and found that the tutorial program significantly enhanced the self-concepts and reading ability of both groups. J. Battle and Meston (1976) found that a camping experience was effective in significantly enhancing the self-concepts of adolescent juvenile delinquent boys. Other investigators (e.g., Miller 1971; Staines 1958) discovered that different approaches within the classroom were effective in elevating self-concepts. For example, Miller (1971), found that homogenous ability grouping was more favorable for the development of academic self-concepts of ability than hetero-genous ability grouping for slow learning boys and girls in grades five and six. J. W. Staines (1958) studied the responses and comments of classroom teachers and their influences on the self-concepts of their children, and found that teachers through their roles as signifi-cant others, can alter the self-concepts of their students by making positive comments to them.

Overwhelming evidence indicates that the self-concept can be enhanced in a posi-tive fashion. Thus, educators, psychologists, and classroom teachers should direct greater energies in this direction, which appears to hold greater promise for assisting children in developing their potential more fully. Programs should be developed that will assist chil-dren in developing more positive views of themselves, which should, in turn, promote academic achievement.

9

REMEDIAL APPROACHES THAT ENHANCE
SELF-ESTEEM AND ACHIEVEMENT

I am of the opinion that most procedures that ensure that the student experience greater degrees of academic success and facilitate the development and maintenance of a more positive teacher-pupil interactive process will enhance the self-esteem of pupils. There are many more techniques and procedures, in addition to the ones cited in this chapter, that can be utilized to enhance achievement and self-esteem of developing children and youth. The particular technique employed is of course, important; but the relationship or interactive process is most crucial. Thus, if a child interacts with a teacher who establishes a positive teacher-pupil interactive process, the child will learn more; and this experience will have a positive effect on his self-esteem. Conversely, if the teacher does not establish a positive teacher-pupil interactive process with the student, the child will learn less, and will not experience significant gains in self-esteem.

In the first section of this chapter we will see a synthesis of approaches that have demonstrated effectiveness in enhancing achievement and self-esteem. We will then go on to offer an instructional strategy which is specifically designed to enhance self-esteem and achievement of learning disabled students.

Remedial Approaches

The following commonly employed approaches have demonstrated their effectiveness for those teaching learning-disabled, hyperkinetic, and underachieving pupils, and for those teaching reading, arithmetic, and spelling.

A. *Teaching the learning-disabled child.*

1. Employ a structured program that emphasizes both oral and written skills.

The mode of expression that is most effective should be used during examinations. All examinations should be untimed.

2. Clarify expectations thoroughly and provide instructions in short, concise sequences.

3. Attempt to facilitate the development of attentional skills by rewarding the child (e.g., permission to participate in self-selected activities, or attention [e.g., "Very good," etc.]) when he is attending appropriately.

4. Encourage the child to read to the class, starting with easy material and increasing the complexity gradually to ensure success and avoid failure.

5. Emphasize positive rather than negative qualities. Create learning experiences to ensure success and reprimand only when absolutely necessary. In instances in which you judge that it is necessary to reprimand, do so as privately and quietly as possible.

6. Permit the child to work in minimal-stimulation environments (e.g., cubicles) when classroom activity impedes attention and concentration.

7. Permit the child to take "time-out" or remove himself from the classroom environment when frustration becomes too great.

B. *Teaching the hyperkinetic child.*

1. Provide an adequate degree of structure for the child and clarify your expectations of him explicitly.

2. Give the child your attention when his behavior is appropriate, and withdraw it when his actions are inappropriate. If his behavior is such that you must intervene, reprimand him as quietly and privately as possible.

3. Provide instructions in short, concise sequences.

4. Attempt to facilitate the development of attentional skills by rewarding the child (e.g., permission to participate in self-selected activities, or attention [e.g., "Very good," etc.]) when he is attending appropriately.

5. Encourage the child to read to the class, starting with easy material and increasing the complexity gradually to ensure success and avoid failure.

C. *Teaching the underachieving child.*

1. Assignments for the underachieving child should be well structured and within his range of achievement level, rather than his ability level.

2. Use older underachievers (fifth and sixth grades) to tutor younger children in the primary grades.

3. Capitalize on the child's interest by enabling him to compete in the area he is interested in.

4. The mode of expression (oral or written) that is most effective should be used during examinations.

5. Use a junior high or high school student to tutor the underachieving elementary school child.

6. Assign grades to the underachiever on the basis of individual effort and production, rather than in relation to the class.

7. If the child needs tutoring outside the school, it should *not* be provided by parents. The child should be encouraged to accept full responsibility for his school work. He should do his own homework on his own. Parents should help only when the child requests help.

8. Create experiences to ensure success.

ENHANCING

9. Avoid retention in school grade, because it rarely benefits the child.
10. Encourage the underachiever to participate in a "study-buddy" system with a friend.
11. Make yourself available to assist underachieving students before or after school. Teachers should make themselves available at least once a week to provide individual assistance for the underachiever.
12. Allow the underachiever to make up incomplete assignments during recess, lunch, or after school.

D. *Teaching the reading-disabled child.*

1. Expose the child to a highly structured, multisensory remedial program.
2. Use large-print books. The larger print tends to be less threatening than standard print.
3. If the child is severely retarded in reading he may need to be placed in a remedial program emphasizing visual, auditory, kinesthetic, and tactile (VAKT) approaches.
4. It is generally recommended that parents do not tutor their child. They should be encouraged, however, to use games to reinforce classroom learning.

E. *Teaching arithmetic to the problem learner.*

1. Provide extensive practice in learning the multiplication table. Later provide similar drill in division.
2. Use money in arithmetic instruction for older children.
3. Use unusual materials in attempts to arouse the child's curiosity regarding basic quantitative concepts, for example: weights and heights, world records, students records, etc.
4. Begin instruction with simple problems initially to ensure an adequate degree of success, which are designed to reduce anxiety regarding arithmetic and build confidence.
5. If the child is severely deficient in arithmetic, start his remedial program at a primary or basic level.
6. Use games in your instructional programs.
7. Use long but simple problems to enhance motivation, for example:

$$\begin{array}{ccc} 888 & 321{,}742{,}134{,}521 & 892{,}678{,}542 \\ -333 & +134{,}151{,}341{,}237 & -151{,}265{,}321 \end{array}$$

8. Encourage parents to play arithmetic games with their children, for example: old maid, chutes and ladders, picture lotto, picture dominoes.

F. *Teaching spelling to the problem learner.*

1. Use the following steps to facilitate recall:
   a. recognition exercises
   b. partial recall
   c. full recall
2. Make assignments short, initially. Increase the length of the word list and complexity of words gradually to ensure an adequate degree of success and motivation.
3. Develop a "star chart" for the child, in which he receives a star when he does as well or better than he did previously.

Alternative Psychotherapeutic Strategies
for the Child Experiencing Adjustment Problems

I have counseled children for more than thirteen years. During this period I have never told a child what he or she should do, but I have successfully encouraged most children to behave in a fashion that I considered to be best for them (that is, to emit behavior that is self-enhancing rather than self-defeating). I was able to assist children effectively because I realized that the most important variable in our interactions with one another is the *relationship*, or the counselor (teacher)-pupil-interactive process. By establishing a highly positive interactive process with the children, I was able to communicate to them that I considered them to be worthy and that my perceptions of their worth were not contingent on their behaving in any prescribed fashion. With this process or relationship established, the children realized that I truly cared for them, respected them, and viewed them as being worthwhile individuals who are capable of making decisions that are important to themselves.

After establishing an effective counselor-(teacher)-pupil-interactive process, the next step in the counseling process is to assist the child in developing a more rational mode of behaving. In order to accomplish this objective, the child is shown that thought (cognition) and emotion (feelings) are closely interrelated; as a consequence, how we feel and subsequently behave is basically determined by how we think. I use an A-B-C paradigm to illustrate this process to the child. This approach is effective because most children—and adults, as well—assume that behavior flows smoothly from A to B to C. For example:

A. Billy calls a client a name.
B. The client becomes angry.
C. The client hits Billy.

When I ask the child "Why did he hit Billy," he will almost always reply that he hit Billy because Billy called him a name that made him angry. I show the child that Billy's name calling did not make him mad; rather, what he told himself at point B (internalized self-verbalizations or thoughts) caused him to become angry, which then resulted in his hitting Billy. I ask the client, "If a much younger child called you the same name, would you become angry and hit him?" The client generally answers "no," because the younger child does not know what he saying or doing. At this point I show the client that the same stimulus existed at A in his interactions with Billy and the younger child: In both instances he was called the same name. When Billy called him the name, he became angry; but he did not become angry when the younger child called him the name. Thus, whether we become angry or not is determined by what we tell ourselves (internalized self-verbalizations) at B, which determines how we will behave at C. If we use rational thought proces-. ses at B (e.g., tell ourselves that an individual's statements regarding us at best represent his perceptions of us and not how we really are), the other individual's behavior will have little effect on how we feel and behave. If the client does not make himself angry at B, by telling himself irrational things, he does not hit Billy and does not have to deal with the negative consequences (e.g., being disciplined by the school principal), which usually occur when pupils fight in the school environment.

By establishing a highly positive counselor (teacher)-pupil-interactive process with the child, and teaching him to think more rationally, I am able to assist him in behaving in a fashion that is basically self-enhancing rather than self-defeating. The child becomes more effective in his interpersonal interactions with others and in dealing with the demands of his environment. He becomes more capable of managing his behavior in a fashion that will be beneficial to himself and to others.

Commentary

A certain degree of academic competence is essential for all children and youth. It is, however, particularly critical for the learning-disabled child. It is essential that educators ensure that the learning-disabled child experience an adequate degree of academic success, which will in turn enhance self-esteem. The following case of a child with a learning disability is presented to illustrate how remediation can improve achievement and in turn enhance self-esteem.

Case Report 9.1: learning disability and low self-esteem.

Homer, J.

9 years, 10 months

Homer was the oldest child in a family comprised of three children. His mother reported that the pregnancy and the birth process were normal, but the client was difficult to manage from the onset. He was "overly active," yelled and screamed frequently, did not sleep well, and didn't enjoy being held or cuddled. With exception of being overly active, development during the first four years was generally normal. Homer walked at 10 months, started to use sentences at 18 months, and was toilet trained at two and a half years.

Homer attended nursery school at the age of four and kindergarten when he was four and a half. His kindergarten teacher described him as a child who possessed a short attention span and predicted that he would experience difficulties in grade one. Homer's parents enrolled him in a bilingual (French-English) program for grade one. He experienced academic difficulties in this setting and subsequently was transferred to a standard public school during his third year. Homer repeated grade three, but this strategy did not help, because he continued to experience severe academic problems during his second year at grade three. At this point Homer was referred to the writer. He was diagnosed as being a child who was experiencing an "attentional deficit disorder with hyperactivity." Intelligence test scores were well within the average range, but the client's self-esteem was low and he was experiencing academic deficits of approximately two years in most areas. An individualized instructional remedial program was developed for Homer which enabled him to make significant academic gains over a two-year period. The client's pre- and posttest scores are presented on the following page.

The Experimental Classroom for Learning-Disabled Pupils

The following program is one I developed after surveying more than 200 researchers and clinicians in Canada and the United States working with children and youth experiencing learning disabilities. It incorporates a consensus of the opinions and strategies of many experts in the field of learning disabilities.

The experimental program is a highly structured individualized one which emphasizes language arts and arithmetic skills. Subject matter is broken down into subskills and taught in short, precise sequences. Both written and oral skills are emphasized, and tasks are arranged systematically, starting with easy material and increasing in complexity gradually to ensure success and avoid failure. The academic and nonacademic programs, as well as selected teaching strategies, are described briefly in the following passage:

Subject Area	June (1976) Grade Score	June (1977) Grade Score	June (1978) Grade Score
Reading	1.3	2.7	5.0
Accuracy	1.7	4.6	5.1
Comp.	1.6	4.1	5.1
Spelling	2.0	2.5	3.8
Arithmetic	2.4	3.8	5.0
IQ (WISC-R)	98	100	106
Self-Esteem	(Score)	(Score)	(Score)
Total	20	33	38
General	8	10	12
Social	4	8	8
School	0	7	9
Parents	8	8	9

I. *Academic program.* The academic program is a highly structured one which emphasizes reading, arithmetic, and language skills. Subjects are taught in 20- to 30-minute blocks. Instructions are precise and presented sequentially with graduated complexity to ensure a reasonable degree of success and minimize failure experiences. Subject matter is broken down into subskills or components, and each subskill in the sequence is mastered before the child moves on to more complex aspects of the program.

II. *Nonacademic program.* The nonacademic program include tasks that are designed to enhance visual-motor perceptual skills, sequencing, eye-hand coordination, and creativity. Subjects taught in this area include art, music, drama, handicrafts, model making, etc. Social games are also used in an attempt to promote interpersonal cooperative skills and awareness of leisure-time recreational pursuits.

Physical education emphasizes movement activities intended to enhance gross- and fine-motor skills. This is a subskill approach, in which activities are broken down into component parts. Throwing a ball, for example, may be broken down into grasping the ball, raising the arm, planting the foot, and releasing the ball. Jumping is broken down into approaching the bar, planting the foot, pushing off, clearing the bar, and landing.

III. *Selected teaching strategies.* Some of the teaching strategies used to individualize instruction in the experimental program are:

1. *Class discussions.* Class discussions are held on the first school day of each week. These discussions are designed to clarify performance objectives and to promote understanding and acceptance of self and others. Interpersonal, communicative skills are discussed; and cooperation and acceptance of all members are emphasized.

2. *Work drum.* A work drum containing individualized assignments is main-

tained in the classroom. The children pick up their assignments each day and begin work immediately.

3. *Work record checklist.* A work record checklist is kept by each child. The teacher marks the checklist at the end of each lesson in order to provide immediate reinforcement. The checklist is also completed by other children when working in groups.

4. Teachers of experimental-class students use a mixture of high- and low-order questions, and ensure that there is a gradual transition from concrete to abstract concepts.

5. Teachers in experimental classes move around the classroom freely, closely monitoring the work of their students.

6. Teachers of experimental subjects handle disruptive behavior in a low-key fashion and when necessary reprimand their students as quietly and privately as possible.

IV. *Teacher-pupil-interactive process.* Positive teacher-pupil interactions are emphasized and maintained at all times. In order to accomplish this, teachers are encouraged to communicate actively to their pupils that they are worthy, significant, and capable, and that this evaluation is not based on any contingencies.

V. *Program specifics.* Instructional levels are established for all students using results derived from standardized achievement test scores. Although the individualized structured instructional program obviously varies for each child, there are similarities in the mode of instruction for each child. For instance, the daily instructional program for each child involves the following:

1. *Language Arts*
   a. Reading equals three 20-minute blocks per day.
      (weekly total equals 300 minutes)
   b. Spelling equals three 20-minute blocks per day.
      (weekly total equals 300 minutes)
   c. Language equals three 20-minute blocks per day.
      (weekly total equals 300 minutes)
   d. Writing equals one 20-minute block per day.
      (weekly total equals 100 minutes)

2. *Arithmetic*
   a. Three 20-minute blocks per day.
      (weekly total equals 300 minutes)

3. *Social Studies*
   a. One 30-minute block per week.
      (weekly total equals 30 minutes)

4. *Science*
   a. One 30-minute block per week.
      (weekly total equals 30 minutes)

5. *Health*
   a. One 30-minute block per week.
      (weekly total equals 30 minutes)

6. *Physical Education*
   a. Two 30-minutes blocks per week.
      (weekly total equals 60 minutes)

7. *Art*
   a. Two 20-minute blocks per week.
      (weekly total equals 40 minutes)
8. *Music*
   a. One 30-minute block per week.
      (weekly total equals 30 minutes)

Individualized instructional techniques are implemented to assist each child in using his/her potential more effectively. Strategies used in the experimental class include:

1. Weekly class discussions are held to discuss assignments and promote greater acceptance and understanding of self and others.
2. The length and degree of complexity of tasks provided for the children are varied gradually to ensure a high degree of success and minimize the probability of failure.
3. A star chart procedure in which the child receives a star when he/she does well or better on tests than he/she did previously is developed for each child.
4. Recognition, partial recall, and full recall exercises are provided to facilitate development of skills.
5. High-interest, low-vocabulary readers are used initially with all subjects, and the degree of vocabulary complexity is adjusted in accord with the degree of progress the subjects makes in reading.
6. Large-print books are used whenever deemed necessary or desireable, because they tend to be less threatening than standard print.
7. Arithmetic instructions begins with simple problems, initially, to ensure an adequate degree of success, which will reduce anxiety regarding arithmetic and build confidence.
8. In arithmetic, unusual materials are used in attempts to arouse children's curiosity regarding basic quantitative concepts, for example, weights and heights, world records, student records, etc.

The program described here has been implemented in selected special education classes for learning-disabled children in a large school system in northwestern Canada. It is hoped that the successes achieved there will provide a model for other, similar programs to be adopted, throughout the next several years, in school systems—public and private—in many places in North America, as a permanent mode of instruction.

Commentary

The importance of academic success on the developing child has been clearly delineated (Battle 1975, 1979). The remedial activities incorporated in the experimental program just described have proven to be effective methods for enhancing achievement and self-esteem. The following case of a twelve-year-old boy is presented as an illustration:

Case Report 9.2: low self-esteem and underachievement.

Rene, J.

12 years

Rene was the youngest in a family of three children. He was the only boy, with sisters aged 13 and 15. His mother stated that the pregnancy, birth process, and early developmental history were normal. Rene walked at 12 months, started to use sentences at 16 months, and was toilet trained at three years, one month.

Rene's mother noted that his problems started when he first entered kindergarten at the age of four and a half. In kindergarten he experienced "seperation anxiety" and cried constantly when his mother attempted to leave the classroom. His mother unfortunately decided to sit outside the door of the classroom to ensure Rene that she would be there if he needed her. When the half day kindergarten class was over, Rene's mother would walk him home. This procedure continued for the first four weeks of kindergarten. After this period, Rene reluctantly agreed to stay in school alone, but insisted that his mother walk him home after the school day was over. This persistence on the part of Rene prevailed when he entered first grade. In addition, he tended to be shy, rarely "mixed" with other children, and on the few occasions when he did play with other children, his profound egocentricity strained social relations. Thus, other children tended to avoid him. Rene experienced severe learning problems throughout his elementary years and was diagnosed as being a child with a "learning disability due to dyslexia." Each year teachers recommended that he repeat his grade, but his parents insisted that he be promoted because they were afraid that failure would have a negative effect on his self-esteem. When Rene was in eighth grade his mother became actively involved in the local chapter of the Association for Parents of Children with Learning Disabilities. It was through her involvement in this organization that she attended a workshop dealing with learning disabilities. She subsequently contacted a psychologist and requested that he interview Rene. He assessed Rene and found him to be a bright child who was underachieving. He was not dyslexic and there were no indications of biological dysfunctioning. The client however, was experiencing severe academic deficits, basically because he had refused to cooperate and use his potential effectively. The psychologist recommended that the parents provide more structure at home for the client. He also recommended that Rene receive individual tutoring in reading, spelling, and arithmetic. In addition, Rene received counseling designed to enhance self-esteem and make him aware of his self-defeating patterns and of the probable consequences of such actions. Rene's pre- and posttest scores are presented on the following page.

Concluding Remarks

There are a number of general approaches which are effective in facilitating the enhancement of self-esteem and achievement. Generally, the most effective strategies for enhancing self-esteem and achievement in children and youth can be categorized under the following:

1. *Teacher-pupil-interactive process.* Teachers should develop a highly positive teacher-pupil-interactive process, a process in which the child learns that:
   a. He is an individual who is worthy and significant.
   b. He is expected to behave and perform in a certain predetermined fashion.
   c. He can choose whether of not to function in that fashion.
   d. He will have to accept the consequences of his actions.
2. *Academic success.* Teachers should ensure that pupils experience a sufficient

Test	June (1979) Grade Score	July (1980) Grade Score	August (1980) Grade Score
Schonell Word Reading	4.5	5.8	6.1
Schonell Word Spelling	3.5	5.2	5.6
Schonell Silent Reading	4.5	8.0	9.3
Bett's Word Recognition	4.5	6.0	6.2
Monroe-Sherman Arith.	5.5	5.9	10.0
IQ (WISC-R)	112	—	114
Self-Esteem	(Score)	(Score)	(Score)
Total	24	31	34
General	9	13	15
Social	4	6	7
School	3	4	4
Parents	8	8	8

degree of academic success. Thus, instructional programs should be developed which will enable pupils to experience an adequate degree of academic success (see Activity B).

3. *Alternative instructional strategies.*
   a. *For the learning disabled.* Children experiencing academic deficits of one and a half years or more in reading and/or arithmetic should be placed in partially integrated special education programs (see Activity F).
   b. *For the gifted.* Children with exceptional general ability and skills should be exposed to instructional strategies which challenge their ability, creativity, and resourcefulness. These children should be permitted to work on self-selected activities after they have completed regularly assigned tasks. These activities should be challenging to the child and should promote creative curiosity.

4. *Alternative psychotherapeutic strategies.*
   a. *For the depressed child.* The depressed child should be referred to his school counselor who should, in turn, subsequently refer him to a psychologist or psychiatrist for psychotherapy.

5. *Parental attitudes.* Parents should provide unconditional, positive regard for their child. That is, they should communicate to the child that he is loved unconditionally. Unconditional, positive regard is a process in which:
   a. The parents communicate to the child that he/she is loved and prized;
   b. This evaluation is not contingent on any predetermined conditions.

Parents are the most powerful source determining the self-esteem of children and youth. Teachers function "in loco parentis," assuming many of the responsibilities of parents during the school day. Thus, how teachers interact with their pupils affect the children's self-esteem. If teachers are to adequately fullfill the goal of education ("develop each child's potential to the fullest"), it is essential that they attend to both the affective and cognitive needs of their pupils. The former is of paramount importance at this particular point in our history because the phenomena of rapid social change has created a high degree of stress in contemporary society. This condition (rapid social change) has resulted in higher rates of divorce, crime, and various forms of psychopathology. For instance, a few decades ago suicide was the fifth highest cause of death among teenagers. Today it is the second highest cause of death among teenagers, second only to auto accidents. Many authorities, however, assume (and rightly so) that many of these auto accidents experienced by teenagers are in reality self-induced accidents. As educators, we are charged with developing the child's potential to the fullest. Thus, in addition to facilitating cognitive competence, we must also attend to the affective needs of the developing child, it we are to produce individuals who are capable of functioning productively in current and future generations. This position is reflected by Snygg and Combs (1959) in the following passage:

> Since the self-concept is a function of experience, what happens to students during their time spent in the educational system must be of vital importance in the development of the phenomenal self. Probably no other agency in our society outside the family has a more profound effect on self . . . . If it is important that students learn to perceive themselves as liked, wanted, acceptable, and responsible, then it follows that education must provide them with the kind of experiences which help them see themselves so and avoid treating them in ways that destroy positive self-feeling (pp. 277-278).

Summary

The remedial approaches reviewed in the chapter have demonstrated effectiveness in assisting children experiencing a wide variety of learning problems to develop their potential more effectively. Strategies discussed in the first section of the chapter include those which have been used successfully to assist the learning-disabled child, the hyperkinetic child, the underachieving child and the reading disabled child. The section also reviews techniques for teaching arithmetic and spelling to the student with learning difficulties.

An experimental program for learning-disabled pupils is delineated in detail in the second section of the chapter.

V

REFERENCES AND INDICES

ENHANCING

REFERENCES

Adler, A. 1927. *The practice and therapy of individual psychology.* New York: Harcourt.

Aichorn, A. 1935. *Wayward youth.* New York: Viking.

Alfert, E. 1958. Two components of assumed similarity. *Journal of Abnormal Social Psychology* 56:119-126.

Allen, V. L., and Feldman, R. S. 1972. Learning through tutoring: low achieving children as tutors. Technical report no. 236. Madison, Wisconsin: University of Wisconsin.

Allport, G. W. 1937. *Personality.* New York: Holt.

Alter, H. M. 1952. A study of high school students with scores of one hundred thirty and above on the California test of mental maturity. Unpublished paper.

Altus, W. D. 1948. A college achiever and nonachiever scale for the Minnesota multiphasic inventory. *Journal of Applied Psychology* 32:385-397.

Amatora, Sr. M. 1957. Validity in self-evaluation. *Educational Psychology Measurement* 16:119-126.

Ames, L. B. 1952. The sense of self of nursery school children as manifested by their verbal behavior. *Journal of Genetic Psychology* 81:193-232.

Anderson, C. C. 1959. The many voices: a preliminary investigation into the consistency of the self-concept. *Alberta Journal of Educational Resources* 5:7-15.

Ansbacher, H. L. 1955. Anomie, the sociologist's concept of lack of social interest. *Journal of Individual Psychology* 20:483-484.

Ansbacher, H. L., and Ansbacher, R. R., eds. 1956. *The individual: psychology of Alfred Adler.* New York: Basic Books.

Aronson, E. 1958. The need for achievement as measured by graphic expression. *Journal of Genetic Psychology* 58:41-49.

Aronson, E. 1972. *The social animal.* San Francisco: Freeman.

Aronson, E., Blaney, N., Sikes, J., Stephan, C., and Snapp, M. 1975. Busing and racial tension: the jigsaw route to learning and liking. *Psychology Today* (February): 43-50.

Aronson, E., and Mills, F. 1959. The effects of severity of initiation on liking for a group. *Journal of Abnormal Social Psychology* 59:177-181.

Atkinson, J. W. 1957. Motivated determinants of risk-taking behavior. *Psychological Review* 64:359-372.

Atkinson, J. W. 1968. The mainspring of achievement oriented activity. In *Learning and the educational process*, ed. J. D. Krumboltz, chapt. 2. Chicago: Rand-McNally.

Atkinson, J. W., and Feather, N. T., eds. 1966. *A theory of achievement motivation.* New York: John Wiley and Sons.

Barrett, H. O. 1956. Underachievement, a possible problem. *The Bulletin* 36:3 p. 111.

Barrett, H. O. 1957. An intensive study of thirty-two children. *Personnel Guidance Journal* 36:192-194.

Barlett, E. W., and Smith, C. P. 1966. Child rearing practices, birth order, and the development of achievement related motives. *Psychological Reports* 19:1207-1216.

Baum, E. L. 1965. The kinetic tutoring project of Washington University. *Liberal Education* 51:551-557.

Battle, J. 1972. The effects of tutoring on self-esteem and achievement. Unpublished doctoral dissertation. Edmonton, Alberta: University of Alberta.

1975. *A comparative study of the self-esteem of deviant and nondeviant students.* Edmonton, Alberta: Edmonton Public Schools.

1976a. *The relationship between intelligence and self-esteem.* Edmonton, Alberta: Edmonton Public Schools.

1976b. *The relationship between teachers' ratings and self-esteem.* Edmonton, Alberta: Edmonton Public Schools.

1976c. Test-retest reliability of the Canadian self-esteem inventory for children (form A). *Psychological Reports* 38:1343-1345.

1977a. The Canadian self-esteem inventory for children. *Test Collection Bulletin* 11:1.

1977b. A comparison of two self-report inventories. *Psychological Reports* 41:159-160.

1977c. Test-retest reliability of the Canadian self-esteem inventory for children (form A). *Psychological Reports* 40:157-158.

1977d. Test-retest reliability of the Canadian self-esteem inventory for adults (form AD). *Perceptual and Motor Skills* 44:38.

1978a. A longitudinal exploratory study of the self-esteem of regular class and special class students. Preliminary findings of a project funded by the Alberta Mental Health Advisory Council.

1978b. The relationship between self-esteem and depression. *Psychological Reports* 42:745-746.

1979a. The Canadian self-esteem inventory for adults (form AD). *News on Tests* (July) 1:6, p. 2.

1979b. The Canadian self-esteem inventory for adults (form AD). *Test Collection Bulletin* (June).

1979c. Self-esteem of students in regular and special classes. *Psychological Reports* 42:212-214.

1980a. The relationship between self-esteem and depression among high school students. *Perceptual and Motor Skills* 51:157-158.

1980b. *A longitudinal comparative study of the self-esteem of regular and special education students.* Edmonton, Alberta: Edmonton Public Schools.

1981. *Culture-free self-esteem inventories for children and adults.* Seattle: Special Child Publications.

Battle, J., and Andriashek, S. 1980. *The effects of partial mainstreaming on the self-esteem of special education students.* Edmonton, Alberta: Edmonton Public Schools.

Battle, J., and Meston. 1976. *The effects that camping have on self-esteem.* Edmonton, Alberta.

Battle, J., Yeudall, L., and Blowers, T. 1980. An exploratory study of self-esteem and brain dysfunction in elementary school children. *Psychological Reports* 46:149-150.

Battle, J., et al. Self-esteem needs of children and youth. Paper presented to the Steering Committee on Students' Needs. Edmonton, Alberta: Edmonton Public Schools.

Beck, A. T., and Beamesderfer, A. 1974. Assessment of depression: depression inventory. In *Psychological measurement in psychopharmacology: modern problems in pharmapsychiatry*, vol. 7, pp. 151-169, ed. P. Pichot. Basel: Karger.

Bee, H. 1975. *The developing child.* New York: Harper and Row.

Beker, J. 1960. The influence of school camping on the self-concepts and social relationships of sixth-grade school children. *Journal of Educational Psychology* 51:352-356.

Bem, D. J. 1972. Self-perception theory. In *Advances in experimental social psychology*, ed. L. Berkowitz, vol. 6. New York: Academic Press.

Bender, R. D., Lewis, K. E., and Schwartz, J. C. 1976. *Talks to jigsaw teachers: a teacher's guide to the implementation of the jigsaw cooperative learning method.*

Berger, C. 1968. Sex differences related to self-esteem factor structure. *Journal of Consulting and Clinicial Psychology* 32:4 pp. 442-446.

Berger, E. M. 1952. The relations between expressed acceptance of self and expressed acceptance of others. *Journal of Abnormal Social Psychology* 47:778-782.

Berger, E. M. 1977. Expressed acceptance of self and others scale. *Test Collection Bulletin* (January).

Berger, I. L., and Sutker, A. R. 1956. The relationship of emotional adjustment and intellectual capacity to academic underachievement of college students. *Mental Hygiene* 40:65-77.

Bergin, A. E. 1962. The effect of dissonant persuasive communications upon changes in self-referring attitude. *Journal of Personality* 30: 423-438.

Berkowitz, P. H., and Rothman, E. P. 1960. *The disturbed child: recognition and psychoeducational therapy in the classroom.* New York: New York University Press.

Bhatnager, K. P. 1966. Academic achievements as a function of one's self-concept and ego functions. *Education and Psychology Review* 6:4 pp. 178-182.

Bills, R. E.

1953. A validation of changes in scores on the index of adjustment and values as measures of changes in emotionality. *Journal of Consulting Psychology* 17: 135-138.

1954. Acceptance of self as measured by interview and the index of adjustment and values. *Journal of Consulting Psychology* 18:22.

1975. *A system for assessing affectivity.* Alabama: University of Alabama Press.

Bills, R. E., Vance, E. L., and McClean, O. S. 1951. An index of adjustment and values. *Journal of Consulting Psychology* 15:257-316.

Bishton, R. 1957. A study of some factors related to achievement of intellectually superior eighth-grade children. *Journal of Educational Research* 51:203-207.

Black, J. 1963. Identification, ego control, and adjusted child development. *Journal of Consulting Psychology* 34:4 pp. 945-953.

Black, W. F. 1974. Self-concept as related to achievement and age in LD children. *Child Development* 4:1137-1140.

Blackham, G. T. 1955. A clinicial study of the personality structures and adjustments of pupils underachieving and overachieving in reading. *Dissertation Abstracts* 15:2 p. 1199.

Blanchard, P. R. 1936. Reading disabilities in relation to difficulties of personality and emotional development. *Mental Hygiene* 20:384-415.

Bledsoe, J. C. 1964. Self-concepts of children and their intelligence, interests, and anxiety. *Journal of Individual Psychology* 20:1 pp. 16-22.

Bodwin, R. F. 1959. The relationship between immature self-concept and certain educational disabilities. *Dissertation Abstracts* 19:1645-1646.

Bourer, R. 1967. Interactive effects of self-esteem and task difficulty on social conformity. *Journal of Personal and Social Psychology* 6:1 pp. 16-22.

Bown, O. 1961. The development of a self-report inventory and its function in a mental health assessment battery. *American Psychologist* 16:402.

Boyce, E. M. 1956. A comparative study of overachieving and underachieving college students on factors other than scholastic aptitude. *Dissertation Abstracts* 16:13 pp. 2088-2089.

Branden, N. 1969. *The psychology of self-esteem.* Los Angeles: Nash Publishing.

Bresee, C. W. 1957. *Affective factors associated with academic underachievement in high school students.*

Bridgham, B. S. Where the loss of talent occurs and why. In College Admission. Volume 7, *The search for talent.*

Brodbeck, A. J., and Perlutter, N. V. 1954. Self-dislike as a determinant of marked in-group/out-group preferences. *Journal of Psychology* 38:271-280.

Brody, N. 1963. Achievement, test anxiety, and subjective probability of success in risk-taking behavior. *Journal of Abnormal Social Psychology* 66:413-418.

Bronfenbrenner, V., Harding, J., and Gallway, M. 1958. The measurement of skill in social perception. In *Talent and society*, ed. D. C. McClelland, A. L. Baldwin, V. Bronfenbrenner, and F. L. Strodtbeck, pp. 29-111. New York: Van Nostrand.

Brookover, W. B., and Gottleib. 1964. *A sociology of education*, 2nd ed. New York: American Book Company.

Brookover, W. B., Paterson, A., and Thomas, S. 1955. The relationship of self-images to achievement in junior high school subjects. Cooperative Research Project no. 845. East Lansing, Michigan: Michigan State University.

Brookover, W. B., Sailor, T., and Paterson, A. 1965. Self-concept of ability and school achievement. *Sociology of Education* 37:271-278.

Brookover, W. B., Thomas, S., and Paterson, A. 1976. An empirical investigation of self-concept in a learning situation. Paper presented before the Ohio Valley Sociological Society (May), East Lansing, Michigan.

Brown, F. G., and Dubois, T. E. 1964. Candidates of academic success for high-ability freshmen. *Personnel Guidance Journal* 42:6 pp. 603-607.

ENHANCING

Brown, H. S. 1941. Investigation of the validity of the MMPI for a college population and the relationship of certain personality traits of achievement. Unpublished doctoral dissertation. Minneapolis: University of Minnesota.

Brown, R. A. 1966. Psychological needs and self-awareness. *Journal of Counseling Psychology* 13:1 pp. 85-88.

Brownfain, J. J. 1952. Stability of the self-concept as a dimension of personality. *Journal of Abnormal and Social Psychology* 47:597-606.

Bruce, P. 1958. Relationship of self-acceptance to other variables with sixth-grade children oriented in self-understanding. *Journal of Educational Psychology* 49:229-238.

Bruck, M., and Bodwin, R. F. 1962. The relationship between self-concept and the presence and absence of scholastic underachievement. *Journal of Clinical Psychology* 19:181-182.

Bruner, J. S., and Caron, A. J. 1959. Cognition, anxiety, and achievement in the preadolescent. Unpublished report. Washington, D. C: Howard University.

Bugental, J. F. T., and Gunning, E. C. 1955. Investigations into self-concepts: stability of reported self-identifications. *Journal of Clinical Psychology* 11:41-46.

Bugental, J. F. T., and Salen, S. L. 1950. Investigations into the self-concept. The W-A-Y technique. *Journal of Personal and Social Psychology* 18:483-498.

Burgess, E. 1956. Personality factors of over- and underachievers in engineers. *Journal of Educational Psychology* 47:88-89.

Butcher, H. J. 1956. A note on the scale product and related methods of scoring attitude scales. *British Journal of Psychology* 47:133-139.

Byrne, D. 1966. *An introduction to personality: a research approach.* Englewood Cliffs, New Jersey: Prentice-Hall.

Byrne, D. E. 1974. *An introduction to personality: research, theory, and applications,* 2nd ed. Englewood Cliffs, New Jersey: Prentice Hall.

Calhoun, S. R. 1956. The effects of counseling on a group of underachievers. *School Review* 64:312-316.

Calvin, A. A. 1953. Adjustment and the discrepancy between self-concept and inferred self. *Journal of Consulting Psychology* 17:39-44.

Canfield, J. and Wells, H. C. 1976. *One hundred ways to enhance self-concept in the classroom: a handbook for teachers and parents.* Englewood Cliffs, New Jersey: Prentice-Hall.

Carlton, L., and Moore, R. H. 1968. *Reading, self-directive dramatization, and self-concept.* Columbus, Ohio: Charles E. Merrill.

Carter, H. D. 1961. Overachievers and underachievers in the junior high school. *California Journal of Educational Resources* 12:51-56.

Castaneda, A., McCandless, B., and Palermo, D. 1956. The children's form of the manifest anxiety scale. *Child Development* 27:327-333.

Chabassal, D. I. 1959. Correlates of academic underachievement in male adolescents. Unpublished doctoral dissertation. Edmonton, Alberta: University of Alberta.

Chance, J. 1961. Independence training and first-graders' achievement. *Journal of Counseling Psychology* 25:2 pp. 149-154.

Chaplin, M. D. 1966. The relationship between self-concept and academic achievement and between level of aspiration and academic achievement. *Dissertation Abstracts* 27:4A pp. 979-980.

Chesler, M. A. 1965. Tutors for disadvantaged youth. *Educational Leadership* 22:559.

Child, I. L., Frank, K. F., and Strom, T. 1956. Self-ratings and Thematic Apperception

Test: their relations to each other and to childhood background. *Journal of Personal and Social Psychology* 25:96-114.

Cicirelli, V. G.

1977a. Purdue self-concept scale for preschool children. *Test Collection Bulletin* (January).

1977b. Purdue self-concept scale for primary grade children. *Test Collection Bulletin* (January).

1977c. Purdue social attitude scales for preschool children. *Test Collection Bulletin* (January).

Clark, E. C. 1961. Factors relating to underachievement. *School and Community* 49:22-23.

Clarke, W. E. 1960. The relationship between college and academic performance and expectancies. Unpublished doctoral dissertation. East Lansing, Michigan: Michigan State University.

Clifford, C., and Wattenburg, W. 1964. Relations of self-concepts to beginning achievement in reading. *Child Development* 35:2 pp. 461-467.

Cloward, R. D.

1967a. Studies in tutoring. *Journal of Experimental Education* 36:14-25.

1967b. The nonprofessional in educational mobilization for youth's tutorial project. *Educational Leadership* 20:604-606.

Cohen, A. R. 1953. The effects of individual self-esteem and situational structure on threat oriented reactions to power. Unpublished doctoral dissertation. Ann Arbor: University of Michigan.

Cohen, A. R. 1957. Some implications of self-esteem for social influence. In *Personality and persuasibility*, ed. C. I. Howland and I. L. Janis, pp. 102-120. New Haven: Yale University Press.

Coleman, J. S. 1961. *The adolescent society.* New York: Free Press.

Coleman, J. S. 1965. The adolescent subculture and academic achievement. In *The schools and the urban crisis*, ed. A. Kerbey and B. Bommouto, pp. 109-120. New York: Holt, Rinehart, and Winston.

Coller, A. R. 1971. The assessment of self-concept in early childhood education. Urbana, Illinois: ERIC ED 057910.

Combs, A. W. 1958. New horizons in field research: the self-concept. *Educational Leadership* 15:315-319.

Combs, A. W., Soper, D. W., and Courson, C. C. 1963. The measurement of self-concept and self-report. *Educational and Psychological Measurement* 23:493-500.

Combs, A. W., and Taylor, C. 1952. Self-acceptance and adjustment. *Journal of Consulting Psychology* 16:89-91.

Combs, C. F. 1963. A study of the relationship between certain perceptions of self and scholastic achievement in academically capable high school boys. *Dissertation Abstracts* 24:63-5034, 620.

Combs, C. F. 1965. Perception of self and scholastic underachievement. In *The schools and the urban crisis*, ed. A. Kerbey and B. Bommouto, pp. 109-120. New York: Holt, Rinehart, and Winston.

Conklins, A. M. 1940. Failure of highly intelligent pupils. *Teachers Contributions to Education* p. 792.

Coopersmith, S.

1959. A method for determining types of self-esteem. *Journal of Abnormal Social*

Psychology 59:87-94.

1962. Clinical explorations of self-esteem. In *Child and education*, proceedings of the 14th International Congress of Applied Psychology, pp. 61-78. Copenhagen: Munksgaard.

1964. The relationship between self-esteem and perceptual constancy. *Journal of Abnormal Social Psychology* 88:217-221.

1967. *Antecedents of self-esteem.* San Francisco: W. H. Freeman.

Corliss, R. B. 1963. Personality factors related to underachievement in college freshmen of high intellectual ability. *Dissertation Abstracts* 24:832.

Cowan, J. C., and Demos, C. D., eds. 1966. *The disadvantaged and potential dropout.* Springfield, Illinois: Charles C Thomas.

Cox, B. G., and Baver, R. A. 1964. The self-confidence and personability in women. *Public Opinion Quarterly* 28:453-466.

Crandall, V. C. 1966. Personality characteristics and social achievement behaviors associated with children's social response tendencies. *Journal of Personal and Social Psychology* 4:477-486.

Crandall, V. C., Dewey, R., Katkowsky, W., and Preston, A. 1963. Parents' attitudes and behaviors and grade school children's academic achievement. *Journal of Genetic Psychology* 53-66, 104.

Crandall, V. C., and Bellugi, U. 1954. Some relationships of interpersonal and intrapersonal conceptualizations to personal-social adjustment. *Journal of Personal and Social Psychology* 23:224-232.

Crary, W. G. 1966. Reactions to incongruent self-experiences. *Journal of Consulting Psychology* 30:3 pp. 246-252.

Cruickshank, W. 1977. Myths and realities in learning disabilities. *Journal of Learning Disabilities* 10:1 pp. 51-58.

Cummings, R. M. P. 1970. A study of the relationship between self-concepts and reading achievement at the third-grade level. Unpublished doctoral dissertation. Birmingham, Alabama: University of Alabama.

Curry, R. L. 1962. The effects of social economic states on the scholastic achievements of sixth-grade children, part one. *British Journal of Educational Psychology* 32:46-49.

Daley, M. E., and Norman, R. D. 1959. The comparative personality adjustment of superior and inferior readers. *Journal of Educational Psychology* 50:31-36.

Davids, A. 1968. Cognitive styles in potential scientists and in underachieving high school students. *Journal of Special Education* 2:2 pp. 197-201.

Davidson, H. H., and Lang, G. 1960. Children's perceptions of their teachers' feelings toward them related to their self-perceptions, school achievement, and behavior. *Journal of Experimental Education* (December) 29:107-118.

Dearborn, W. F. 1949. The student's background in relation to school success. In *Guidance conference on the measurement of student adjustment and achievement*, ed. M. Wilna and T. Donahue, pp. 191-200. Ann Arbor: University of Michigan Press.

Dechant, E. 1968. *Diagnosis and remediation of reading disability.* West Nyack, New York: Parker.

D' Heurle, E. A., Jeanne, C., and Haggard, E. 1959. Personality, intellectual and achievement patterns in gifted children. *Psychological Monographs* 73:13 (whole no. 483).

Diener, D. L. 1960. Similarities between overachieving and underachieving students. *Per-*

sonnel Guidance Journal 38:5 pp. 396-400.

Diller, L. 1954. Conscious and unconscious self-attitudes after success and failure. *Journal of Personal and Social Psychology* 23:1-12.

Dittes, J. E.

    1959a. Attractiveness of group as a function of self-esteem and acceptance by group. *Journal of Abnormal Social Psychology* 59:77-82.

    1959b. Effects of changes in self-esteem upon impulsiveness and deliberation in making judgments. *Journal of Abnormal Social Psychology* 58:348-356.

Dollar, B. 1974. *Learning and growing through tutoring.* New York: National Commission on Resources for Youth.

Dorsey, J., and Seegers, W. 1959. *Seeing consciously: the science of self.* Detroit: Wayne State University Press.

Douvan, E. 1956. Social status and success striving. *Journal of Abnormal Social Psychology* 52:219-223.

Dow, M., Herringhaust, M. J., and Robinson, M. 1946. The development of the ideal self in childhood and adolescence. *Journal of Educational Research* 40:241-257.

Dowd, R. J. 1952. Underachieving students of high capacity. *Journal of Higher Education* 23:327-333.

Dreikurs, R., Grunwald, B. B., and Pepper, F. C. 1971. *Maintaining sanity in the classroom; illustrated teaching techniques.* New York: Harper and Row.

Drews, E. M., and Teaham, J. E. 1957. Parental attitudes and academic achievers. *Journal of Clinical Psychology* 13:328-332.

Dribbs, J. M., Jr. 1964. Self-esteem communicator characteristic and attitude change. *Journal of Abnormal Social Psychology* 69:2 pp. 173-181.

Dudek, S. Z., and Lester, E. P. 1968. The good-child facade in chronic underachievers. *American Journal of Orthopsychiatry* 38:1 pp. 153-160.

Duel, H. J. 1958. Effect of periodical self-evaluation on student achievement. *Journal of Educational Psychology* 49:197-199.

Duff, O. L., and Siegel, L. 1960. Biographic factors associated with academic over- and underachievement. *Journal of Educational Psychology* 51:1 pp. 43-46.

Dulton, B. E. 1962. The use of the parent attitude research inventory with the parents of bright academic underachievers. *Journal of Educational Psychology* 53:5 pp. 203-208.

Dun, W. K., and Schmatz, R. R. 1964. Personality differences between high achievers and low achievers in gifted children. *The Reading Teacher* 17:251-254.

Easton, J. 1960. Some personality traits of underachieving and achieving school students of superior ability. *Psychological Abstracts* 34:7786.

Eisenberg, L. 1966. In *The disabled reader*, p. 8. Baltimore: John Hopkins University Press.

Engel, M. 1959. The stability of the self-concept in adolescence. *Journal of Abnormal Social Psychology* 58:211-215.

Erikson, E. H. 1959. *Growth and crises: psychological issues.* New York: International University Press.

Feather, N. T. 1963. The effects of differential failure on expectations of success, repeated anxiety, and response uncertainty. *Journal of Personal and Social Psychology* 31: 289-312.

Feather, N. T. 1965. The relationship of expectation of success to need achievement and test anxiety. *Journal of Personal and Social Psychology* 1:118-126.

Federal Register. 1976. (Thursday, December 20) 41:252 pp. 56966-56998.

Feld, S., and Lewis, J. 1957. Further evidence on the stability of the factor structure of the test anxiety scale for children. *Journal of Consulting Psychology* 31:434.

Feld, S., Owen, W., and Sorenson, S. B. 1963. Interviews with parents of anxious and defensive young boys. Unpublished paper. Washington, D. C.: National Institute of Mental Health.

Fergen, L. M., and Oden, M. 1940. Status of the California gifted group at the end of 16 years. In *Intelligence, its nature and nurture*, 39th Yearbook of the National Society for the Study of Education, pp. 67-84. Bloomington: Public School Pub.

Fey, W. F.

    1955. Acceptance by others and its relationship to acceptance of self and others. *Journal of Abnormal Social Psychology* 50:274-276.

    1957. Correlates of certain subjective attitudes towards self and others. *Journal of Clinical Psychology* 13:44-49.

    1959. Acceptance of self and others, and its relation to therapy readiness. *Journal of Clinical Psychology* 10:269-271.

Fine, B. 1957. *The underachievers, how they can be helped.* New York: E. P. Dutton.

Fink, M. B. 1962. Self-concept as it relates to academic underachievement. *California Journal of Educational Research* 13:57-62.

Fisher, J. K., and Waetjen, W. B. 1966. An investigation of the relationship between the separation by sex of eighth-grade boys and girls, and english achievements and self-concepts. *Journal of Educational Press* 59:9 pp. 409-412.

Fitts, W. 1964-65. *Manual for the Tennessee self-concept scale.* Nashville, Tennessee: Counsellor Recording and Tests.

Flanagan, J. C. 1964. Product talent. Cooperative Research Project no. 635, final report. Washington, D. C.: U.S. Office of Education.

Fleming, E., and Wonderley, D. M. 1965. Underachievement and the intelligent child. *Exceptional Children* 31:8 pp. 405-409.

Ford, T. R. 1967. Social factors affecting academic performance: further evidence. *Social Review* 65:415-422.

Frager, S., and Stern, C. 1970. Learning by teaching. *The Reading Teacher* 23:5 pp. 403-406.

Fraiser, A. J., and Combs, A. W. 1958. New horizons in field research: the self-concept. *Educational Leadership* 15:305-319.

Frank, J. D. 1935. Some psychological determinants of the level of aspiration. *American Journal of Psychology* 47:285-293.

Frank, L. K. 1955. *Individual development.* New York: Doubleday.

Frankel, E. A. 1960. Cooperative study of achieving and underachieving high school boys of high intellectual ability. *Journal of Educational Research* 53:172-180.

Freedburg, N. E., and Payne, D. T. 1967. Parental influence on cognitive development in early childhood: a review. *Child Development* 38:65-78.

Fromm, E. 1941. *Escape from freedom.* New York: Rinehart.

Fromm, E. 1947. *Man for himself.* New York: Rinehart.

Gadzella, B. M., and Fournet, G. P. 1976. Student self-rating scale of excellence. *Test Collection Bulletin* 10:3.

Gaier, E. L. 1961. Student self-esteem of final course grades. *Journal of Genetic Psychology* 98:63-67.

Galloway, J. R., Schipper, W. U., and Wilson, W. C. 1976. *Directory of learning disabilities services for state education agencies.* Washington, D. C.: National Association of State Directors of Special Education.

Gann, E. 1945. *Reading difficulty and personality organization.* New York: King Press.

Gardner, J. W. 1961. *Excellence can be equal and excellent too.* New York: Harper and Row.

Gartner, A., Kohler, M. C., and Riessman, F. 1971. *Children teach children: learning by teaching.* New York: Harper and Row.

Gates, A. I. 1941. The role of personality: maladjustment in reading disability. *Pedagogical Seminary and Journal of Genetic Psychology* 59:77-83.

Gergen, K. J., and Bauer, R. A. 1967. Interactive effects of self-esteem and task difficulty on social conformity. *Journal of Personal and Social Psychology* 6:1 pp. 16-22.

Gerhart, G., Gary, G., and Hoyt, D. P. 1958. Personality needs of underachieving freshmen. *Journal of Applied Psychology* 42:125-128.

Gerrard, H. B. 1958. Some effects of involvement upon evaluation. *Journal of Abnormal Social Psychology* 57:118-120.

Gibbs, D. N. 1965. Student failure and social maladjustment. *Personnel Guidance Journal* 43:6 pp. 530-585.

Gilbert, G. G., and Hoyt, D. P. 1958. Personality needs of under- and overachieving freshmen. *Journal of Applied Psychology* 42:125-128.

Gillman, G. B. 1969. The relationship between self-concept, intellectual ability, achievement, and manifest anxiety among select groups of Spanish-surname migrant students in New Mexico. ERIC ED 029732. Unpublished doctoral dissertation. Albuquerque, New Mexico: University of New Mexico.

Gilmore, J. O. 1952. A new venture in the testing of motivation. *College Board Review* 15:221-226.

Giuliani, G. A. 1968. The relationship of self-concept and verbal mental ability to levels of reading readiness among kindergarten children. *Dissertation Abstracts International* 28 (9-B): 3866.

Goldenberg, M. 1959. A three-year experimental program at Dewitt Clinton high school to help bright underachievers. New York: High Points Board of Education of the City of New York.

Gollob, H. G., and Dittes, J. E. 1965. Effects of manipulated self-esteem on persuasability depending on threat and complexity of communication. *Journal of Personal and Social Psychology* 2:2 pp. 195-201.

Gordon, A., and Gergen, K., eds. 1968. *Classic and contemporary perspectives.* The Self in Social Interaction, vol. 1. New York: John Wiley and Sons.

Gordon, A., and Nisbett, R. E. 1967. Self-esteem and susceptibility to social influence. *Journal of Personal and Social Psychology* 5:3 pp. 268-276.

Gottesman, T. 1963. Heritability of personality. *Psychological Monographs* 77:8 pp. 1-21.

Gough, H. G.
    1946. The relationship of socioeconomic states to personality inventory and achievement test records. *Journal of Educational Psychology* 37:527-540.
    1949. Factors relating to academic achievement of high school students. *Journal of Educational Psychology* 40:65-78.
    1953. What determines the academic achievement of high school students. *Journal of Educational Research* 46:321-331.

Gough, H. G., and Heilbrun, A. B., Jr. 1965. *The adjective checklist manual.* Palo Alto, California: Consulting Psychologists Press.

Gowan, J. C. 1957. Dynamics of the underachievement of gifted students. *Exceptional Children* 24:98-101.

Grant, J. F. 1966. A longitudinal program of individualized instruction in grades four, five, and six. Unpublished master's thesis. Berkeley, California: University of California.

Granzow, K. R. 1954. A comparative study of underachievers, normal achievers, and overachievers in reading. *Dissertation Abstracts* 14:1 pp. 631-632.

Guertin, W. H., and Jourard, S. M. 1962. Characteristics of the real-self/ideal-self, discrepancy scores revealed by factor analysis. *Journal of Consulting Psychology* 26: 241-245.

Gurin, G. 1960. The use of the native apperception to assess motivation in a nationwide interview study. *Psychological Monographs* 74:12 (whole no. 449).

Gust, C. T., Wrinkler, R. C., Menger, P. C., and Teriglad, J. J. 1963. Changes in the concepts of self-esteem and others of NDEA Guidance Institute members. *Journal of Counseling Psychology* 3:227-231.

Gustav, A. 1962. Comparison of college grades and self-concept. *Psychological Reports* 11:2 pp. 601-602.

Guttentag, M. D., and Mark, G. 1966. The effects of college attendance on mature women: changes in self-concept and evaluation of student role. *Journal of Social Psychology* 69:1 pp. 55-58.

Haggard, E. A. 1957. Socialization, personality, and academics in gifted children. *School Review* 65:388-414.

Hamacheck, D. E., ed. 1965. *The self in growth, teaching, and learning.* Englewood Cliffs, New Jersey: Prentice-Hall.

Hamacheck, D. E. 1971. A study of the relationship between certain measures of growth and self-images of elementary school children. *Dissertation Abstracts* vol. 1.

Havighurst, R. J., Robinson, M. Z., and Dorr, M. 1946. The development of the ideal self in childhood and adolescence. *Journal of Educational Research* 40:241-257.

Heck, L. H. 1967. *The anatomy of achievement motivation.* New York: Academic Press.

Helmrich, R., Stapp, J., and Ervin, C. 1976. Texas social behavior inventory. *Test Collection Bulletin* 10:3.

Henlon, T. E., Hoftstaetter, P. R., and O'Conner, J. P. 1954. Congruence of self and ideal self in relation to personality adjustment. *Journal of Consulting Psychology* 18: 215-218.

Herbart, E., Gelfand, D. M., and Hartman, D. P. 1969. Imitation and self-esteem as determinants of self-critical behavior. *Child Development* 40:421.

Hobbs, N., ed. 1975. *Issues in the classification of children,* vol. 1. San Francisco: Jossey-Bass.

Hoffman, M. 1963. Child-rearing practices and moral development: generalizations from empirical research. *Child Development* 34:295-318.

Holland, J. K. 1959. The prediction of college grades from the California psychological inventory and the scholastic aptitude test. *Journal of Educational Psychology* 50:4 pp. 135-142.

Holland, J. K. 1961. Creative and academic performance among talented adolescents. *Journal of Educational Psychology* 52:3 pp. 136-147.

Horan, J. 1965. Project literacy. *National Catholic Educational Association Bulletin* 62: 506.

Horney, K.

    1936: Culture and neurosis. *American Social Review* 221-230.

    1937. *The neurotic personality of our time.* New York: W. W. Norton.

    1939. *New Ways in psychoanalysis.* New York: W. W. Norton.

1945. *Our inner conflicts.* New York: W. W. Norton.

1950. *Neurosis and human growth.* New York: W. W. Norton.

Horrall, B. 1957. Academic performance and personality adjustments of highly intelligent college students. *Genetic Psychology Monographs* 55:3-83.

Iscoe, I. 1959. Probationers and honor students. *University of Texas Arts and Sciences* 3: 2 pp. 1-5.

Jacobson, E. 1954. The self and the object world. *Psychoanalytical Studies of the Child* 9:75-128.

James, W. 1890. *Principles of psychology*, in 2 vols. New York: Holt.

Janis, I. L. 1954. Personality correlation of susceptibility to persuasion. *Journal of Personal and Social Psychology* 22:505-518.

Janis, I. L. 1955. Anxiety indicates relations to susceptibility and persuasion. *Journal of Abnormal Social Psychology* 51:663-667.

Janis, I. L., and Field, P. B. 1959. Sex differences and personality factors related to persuasibility. In *Personality and persuasibility*, ed. C. I. Howland and I. L. Janis, pp. 102-120. New Haven, Connecticut: Yale University Press.

Janowitz, G. 1965. *Helping hands: volunteer work in education*, p. 8. Chicago: University of Chicago Press.

Jason, M. H., and Dubnow, B. 1973. The relationship between self-perception of reading abilities and reading achievement. In *Assessment problems in reading*, ed. W. H. MacGinitie, pp. 96-101. Newark, Delaware: International Reading Association.

Jersild, A. T. 1952. *In search of self.* New York: Bureau of Publications, New York Teachers College.

Jersild, A. T. 1960. *Child psychology*, 5th ed. Englewood Cliffs, New Jersey: Prentice-Hall.

Jonietz, A. L. 1959. A study of achieving and nonachieving students of superior ability. Unpublished report. Chicago: University of Illinois.

Jourard, S. M., and Secord, P. 1954. Body size and body cathexis. *Journal of Consulting Psychology* 18:184.

Kagan, J., and Moss, H. S. 1961. Personality and social development: family and peer influences. *Review of Educational Research* 31:5 pp. 463-474.

Kagan, J., and Moss, H. S. 1961. The availability of conflicted ideas: a neglected parameter in assessing projective test responses. *Journal of Personal and Social Psychology* 29:217-234.

Kagan, J., and Moss, H. S. 1962. *Birth to maturity.* New York: Wiley.

Kahl, J. A. 1953. Education aspiration of common boys. *Harvard Educational Review* 23: 186-203.

Karner, M. B. 1963. The efficiency of two organizational plans for underachieving gifted children. *Exceptional Children* 29:438-446.

Katz, F. M. 1964. The meaning of success: some differences in value systems of social classes. *Journal of Social Psychology* 62:141-148.

Keil, W., and Sader, M. 1968. Situations: specifische einfleuesse auf die fiestungsmotivation ach heckhausen. *Zeitschrift fuer Experimentelle und Angewandte Psychology* 15:1 pp. 100-121.

Keinowitz, R. F., and Ansbacher, H. L. 1960. Personality and achievement in mathematics. *Journal of Individual Psychotherapy* 16:84-87.

Kelly, G. 1970. Personal construct theory. In *Reading for a cognitive theory of personality*, ed. J. Mancusso. New York: Holt, Rinehart, and Winston.

Kempf, E. J. 1921. *The autonomic functions and the personality.* Nervous and Mental Disorders Monograph no. 28.

Kephart, N. C. 1960. *The slow learner in the classroom.* Columbus, Ohio: Charles E. Merrill.

Keshian, J. G. 1961. Why children succeed in reading: a study to determine in three selected communities, some of the common physical, social, emotional characteristics and experiences of children who learn to read. Unpublished doctoral dissertation. New York: New York University.

Keshian, J. G. 1962. Is there a personality pattern common to successful readers? *Elementary English* 39:229-230.

Kimball, B. 1952. The sentence completion technique in a study of scholastic underachievement. *Journal of Consulting Psychology* 16:353-358.

Kimball, B. 1953. Case studies of educational failure during adolescence. *American Journal of Orthopsychiatry* 16:213-216.

Kirsch, J. M. 1968. A comparative study of patterns of underachievement among male college students. *Dissertation Abstracts* 28(8B):3461-3462.

Knapp, R. H. 1959. *Guidance in the elementary school.* Boston: Allyn and Bacon.

Kohn, A. R., and Felder, F. E. 1961. Age and differences in the perception of persons. *Sociometry* 24:157-163.

Kohn, M. L., and Carroll, E. E. 1960. Social class and allocation of parents' responsibilities. *Sociometry* 23:272-392.

Kokovich, S. 1970. A study of the relationship between perceptions of leadership behavior and certain dimensions of teacher morale. *Dissertation Abstracts International* 31 (3-A).

Kornich, M. 1965. *Underachievement.* Springfield, Illinois: Charles C Thomas.

Krippner, S. 1961. The vocational preference of high achieving and low achieving junior high school students. *Gifted Children Quarterly* 588-590.

Kris, E. 1950. *Psychoanalytic explorations in art.* New York: International University Press.

Krugmar, M. 1960. Identification and preservation of talent. *Teacher College Record* 51:459-563.

Kurtz, J. J., and Swenson, E. J. 1951. Factors related to overachievement and underachievement in school. *School Review* 59:472-480.

Lacks, P. B., and Powell, B. J. 1970. The Mini-Mult as a personnel screening technique: preliminary report. *Psychological Reports* 27:909-910.

Labenne, W. D., and Green, B. I. 1969. *Educational implications of self-concept theory.* Pacific Palisades, California: Goodyear Publishing.

LaForge, R., and Suczek, R. 1955. The interpersonal dimension of personality, part 3: an interpersonal checklist. *Journal of Personal and Social Psychology* 24:94-112.

Lamy, M. L. 1964. Relationship of self-concept of early primary children to achievement in reading. In *Human development: readings in research*, ed., I. Gordon. Glenview, Illinois: Scott, Foresmann.

Larsen, H., and Noelfren, I. 1962. Un lang und entwickling der leistungs motivation (I) in wetteiffer der kleinkinds. *Psychology Forsch* 26:313-339.

Larsen, H. 1965. *The anatomy of achievement motivation.* New York: Academic Press.

Larsen, S. C., Parker, R., and Jorjorian, S. 1973. Differences in self-concept of normal and learning disabled children. *Perceptual and Motor Skills* 37:510.

Lasswell, H. 1930. *Psychopathology and politics.* Chicago: University of Chicago Press.

Layton, E. 1954. A study of the factors associated with failure in the ninth grade of the Hempstead high school. *Microfilm Abstracts* 14:1 p. 67.

Lecky, P. 1945. *Self-consistency, a theory of personality.* Fort Meyers Beach, Hawaii: Island Press.

Leibman, O. B. 1954. The relationship of personal and social adjustment to academic achievement in the elementary school. *Dissertation Abstracts* 14:1 p. 67.

Leonetti, R. 1973. A primary self-concept scale for Spanish-surnamed children, grades K-4. Unpublished doctoral dissertation. Las Cruces, New Mexico: New Mexico State University, ERIC ED 071-813.

Leslie, L. 1975. Susceptibility to interference effects in short-term memory of normal and retarded readers. *Perceptual and Motor Skills* 40:3 pp. 791.

Lewin, K., Dembo, T., Festinger, L., and Sears, P. S. 1944. Level of aspiration. In *Personality and behavior disorders*, vol. 1, ed. M. J. and M. C. V. Hunt, pp. 333-378. New York: Ronald.

Lewin, P. 1965. Tutoring program. *School Management* 9:126.

Lewis, R. W. 1974. The relationship of self-concept to reading achievement. Unpublished doctoral dissertation. University of Virginia. *Dissertation Abstracts* 34:3859-A; University Microfilms no. 73-31, 141.

Lewis, W. D. 1940. *A study of superior children in elementary school.* Contributions to Education, no. 266. New York: George Peabody College for Teachers.

Lewis, W. D. 1941. Comparative study of the personalities, interests, and home backgrounds of gifted children of superior and inferior intellectual achievement. *Pedagogical Seminary and Journal of Genetic Psychology* 59:207-218.

Lightfoot, C. G. 1951. *Personality characteristics of bright and dull children.* New York: Bureau of Publications, Columbia University.

Lipton, C. 1963. Cultural heritage and the relationship to self-esteem. *Journal of Educational Sociology* 36:23-212.

Long, B., Henderson, E. H., and Ziller, R. C. 1967. Developmental changes in the self-concept during middle childhood. *Merrill-Palmer Quarterly of Behavior and Development* 13:201-215.

Long, B., Ziller, R. C., and Henderson, E. H. 1968. Developmental changes in the self-concept during adolescence. *School Review* 76:210-230.

Lumpkin, D. D. 1959. Relationship of self-concept to achievement in reading. *Dissertation Abstracts* 20:204-205.

Lundin, R. W. 1966. *Personality.* Dubuque, Iowa: William C. Brown.

Mackler, B., and Giddings, M. C. 1965. Cultural deprivation: a study of mythology. *Teachers College Record* 66:668-713.

Mahone, C. H. 1960. Fear of failure and unrealistic vocational aspiration. *Journal of Abnormal Social Psychology* 60:253-261.

Mallet, S. 1957. *A history of the University of Oxford.* Oxford: Oxford University Press.

Matine, J. G. 1956. Relationship between the self-concept and difference in the strength and generality of achievement motivation. *Journal of Personal and Social Psychology* 24:364-375.

Maslow, A. H. 1935. The dominance drive as a determiner of social behavior in infra-human primates. *Psychology Bulletin* 32:714-715.

Mason, B. C. 1961. Family structure and achievement motivation. *American Sociology Review* 26:574-585.

Mason, E. P. 1954. Some factors in self-judgments of the aged. *Journal of Gerontology* 9:324-337.

Matthews, T. H. 1956. Academic failures. Canadian crises in higher education. National

Conferences of Canadian Universities.

Matteson, R. W. 1956. Self-estimates of college freshmen. *Personnel Guidance Journal* 34:280-284.

McClelland, D. C. 1958. Risk-taking in children with low and high need for achievement. M. J. W. Atkinson, pp. 306-321.

McClelland, D. C., Atkinson, M. J. W., Clark, R. A., and Lowell, E. L. 1953. *The achievement motive.* New York: Appleton-Century-Crofts.

McClosky, M., and Kleinbard, P. 1974. *Youth into adult.* New York: National Commission on Resources for Youth.

McGuire, C. 1960. The prediction of talented behavior in the junior high school. In *Educational Testing Service Proceedings.* International Conference on Testing Problems, Princeton, New Jersey.

McKee, J. P., and Sheriffs, A. C. 1957. The differential evaluation of males and females. *Journal of Personal and Social Psychology* 25:356, 371.

McKenzie, J. D. 1961. An attempt to develop scales predictive of academic over- and underachievement. *Dissertation Abstracts* 22:1 p. 632.

McKenzie, J. D. 1964. The dynamics of deviate achievement. *Personnel Guidance Journal* 42:683-686.

Mead, G. H. 1934. *Mind, self, and society.* Chicago: University of Chicago Press.

Merrill, R. M., and Murphy, D. T. 1959. Personality factors and academic achievements in college. *Journal of Counseling Psychology* 50:66-69.

Mettee, D. R., Williams, A., and Reed, H. D. 1972. Facilitating self-image enhancement and improving reading performance in young Black males. Unpublished paper. New Haven, Connecticut: Yale University.

Middleton, G., and Guthrie, G. M. 1959. Personality syndromes and academic achievement in college. *Journal of Educational Psychology* 50:66-69.

Miles, C. C. 1954. Gifted children. In *Normal child psychology*, 2nd ed., ed. L. Carmichael, pp. 984-1063. New York: Wiley.

Miller, B. P. 1971. A study of the relationship among student self-concept, teacher image, and ability grouping. *Dissertation Abstracts International* 31 (8-A): 3966-3907.

Miller, L. M., ed. 1962. *Guidance for the underachiever with superior ability.* Bulletin no. 25, OE 25021. Washington, D. C.: U.S. Department of Health, Education, and Welfare.

Miskimims, R. W., and Braucht, G. 1971. *Description of the self.* Fort Collins, Colorado: Rocky Mountain Behavioral Science Institute (P. O. Box 2037).

Mitchell, J. V. 1959. Goal-setting behavior as a function of self-acceptance, over- and underachievement, and related personality variables. *Journal of Educational Psychology* 50:3 pp. 93-104.

Miyomoto, S. F., and Dornbusch, S. M. 1956. A test of interactionist hypotheses of self-conception. *American Journal of Sociology* 61:339-403.

Money, J. 1966. *The disabled reader: education of the dyslexic child.* Baltimore: Johns Hopkins University Press.

Moore, W. G. 1965. *The tutorial system and its future.* Oxford: Pergamon Press.

Morgan, H. H. 1952. A psychometric comparison of achieving and nonachieving college students of high ability. *Journal of Consulting Psychology* 16:292-298.

Morse, S., and Gergen, K. 1970. Social comparison, self-consistency, and the self-concept. *Journal of Personal and Social Psychology* 16:292-298.

Morrow, W. R., and Wilson, R. C.

    1961a. Family relationships of bright, high achieving and underachieving high school boys. *Child Development* 32:3 pp. 501-510.

    1961b. School and career adjustment of bright, high achieving and underachieving high school boys. *Journal of Genetic Psychology* 101:91-103.

    1961c. The self-reported personal and social adjustment of bright, high achieving and underachieving high school boys. *Journal of Child Psychology and Psychiatry* 2:203-209.

Moustakas, C. E. 1956. *The self-exploration in personal growth.* New York: Harper and Row.

Muller, D. G., and Leonetti, R.

    1974a. *Primary self-concept inventory technical report.* Austin, Texas: Learing Concepts.

    1974b. *Primary self-concept inventory test manual.* Austin, Texas: Learning Concepts.

Murphy, L. B. 1937. *Social behavior and child personality.* New York: Columbia University Press.

Nash, L. 1964. A study of particular self-perceptions as related to scholastic achievement of junior high school age pupils in a middle class community. *Dissertation Abstracts* 124:9 p. 3837.

Nason, L. J. 1958. *Academic achievement of gifted high school children.* University of Southern California Education Monograph Service, no. 17. Los Angeles: University of Southern California.

Nettler, G. 1957. A measure of alienation. *American Sociology Review* 22:670-677.

New York Board of Education. 1959. Office of Educational Research. New York, NY.

Norris, G., Krug, H., and Krug, D. 1975. Placement in regular programs: procedures and results. *Exceptional Children* 41:413-417.

Nunnally, J. C. 1975. The study of change in evaluation research: principles concerning measurement, experimental design, an analysis. In *Handbook of evaluation research*, ed. E. L. Struening and M. Guttentog, pp. 106-107. Beverly Hills, California: Sage.

Nuthmann, A. 1957. Conditioning of a response class on a personality test. *Journal of Abnormal Social Psychology* 54:19-23.

Owens, W. A., and Johnson, W. 1955. Some measured personality traits of college students. *Dissertation Abstracts* 15:3 pp. 2104-2105.

Pahordy, J. M. 1969. For Johnny's reading sake. *The Reading Teacher* 22:8 pp. 720-724.

Pearlman, S. 1952. An investigation of academic underachievement among intellectually superior college students. *Dissertation Abstracts* 12:1 p. 599.

Perlmutter, H. V. 1954. Relations between the self-image, the image of the foreigner, and the desire to live abroad. *Journal of Psychology* 38:131-137.

Perkins, H. V.

    1958a. Factors influencing change in children's self-concepts. *Child Development* 29:221-230.

    1958b. Teachers' and peers' perceptions of children's self-concepts. *Child Development* 29:203-220.

Perschal, E. 1960. *Encourage the excellent.* New York: The Fund for the Advancement of Education.

Phillips, E. L. 1951. Attitudes toward self and others: a brief questionaire report. *Journal of Consulting Psychology* 15:79-81.

Pierce, J. V.

1961a. Personality and achievement among high school boys. *Journal of Individual Psychology* 17:102-107.

1961b. *Sex differences in achievement motivation of able high school students.* Quincy, Illinois: University of Chicago, Quincy Youth Development Project.

Pierce, J. V., and Brown, P. H. 1960. Motivation patterns of superior high school students. In *the gifted student.* Cooperative Research Monograph, no. 2. Washington, D. C.: Superintendent of Documents, U.S. Government Printing Office.

Piers, E. V. 1969. *Manual for the Piers-Harris self-concept scale (the way I feel about myself).* Nashville, Tennessee: Counselor Recording and Tests.

Piers, E. V., and Harris, D. B. 1964. Age and other correlates of self-concept in children. *Journal of Educational Psychology* 55:91-95.

Postman, N., and Weingarten, C. 1969. *Teaching as a subversive activity.* New York: Delacorte Press.

Powell, W. J., and Jourard, S. M. 1963. Some objective evidence of immaturity in under-achieving college students. *Journal of Counseling Psychology* 10:3 pp. 276-282.

Prince, M. 1924. *The unconscious,* 2nd ed. New York: Macmillan.

Purkey, W. W. 1970. *Self-concept and school achievement.* Englewood Cliffs, New Jersey: Prentice-Hall.

Quandt, I. J. 1973. Relationships among reading, self-concept, first-grade reading achieve-ment, and behaviors. Microfilm. Ann Arbor, Michigan: University Microfilm.

Racet, J. 1936. *La naissence de l'intelligence chez enfant.* Neuchatel, Paris: Delachaux et Niestle.

Radke, M., Trager, H. G., and Davis, H. 1949. Social perceptions and attitudes of children. Monograph. *Genetic Psychology* 40:327-477.

Ralph, J. B. 1966. *Bright underachievers: Horace-Mann.* New York: Lincoln Institute of School Experiment.

Rasmussen, C., and Zender, A. 1954. Group membership and self-evaluation. *Human Relations* 7:239-251.

Ratchick, J. 1955. Achievement and capacity: a comparative study of pupils with low achievement and high intelligence quotients, with pupils of high achievement and intelligence quotients, in a selected New York City high school. *Dissertation Abstracts* 15:3 p. 2106.

Redder, T. A. n.d. A study of some relationships between the level of self-concept, academic achievement, and classroom adjustment. Unpublished doctoral disser-tation. Denton, Texas: North Texas State College.

Regensburg, J. *Studies of educational success and failure in super-normal children.* Ar-chives of Psychology, no. 129, ed. M. R. S. Woodworth. New York: Columbia University Press.

Riessman, F. 1965. It's time for a moon shot in education. Paper presented at the Cali-fornia Advisory Council on Educational Research, Los Angeles.

Ritter, J., and Thorn, A. 1954. *Methods of teaching in town and rural schools.* New York: Dryden Press.

Roberts, H. 1962. Factors affecting the academic underachievement of bright high school students. *Journal of Educational Research* 56:176-183.

Robinowitz, R. 1956. Attributes of pupils achieving beyond their level of expectancy. *Journal of Personal and Social Psychology* 24:308-317.

Robinson, M. F., and Freeman, W. 1954. *Psycho-surgery and the self.* New York: Grune and Stratton.

Robinson, J. P., and Shaver, P. R. 1976. *Measures of social-psychological attitudes*, 4th ed. Ann Arbor, Michigan: Institute for Social Research, University of Michigan.

Robinson, W. P. 1962. An experiment to investigate the relationship between a level of aspiration and achievement in academically successful and unsuccessful boys. Unpublished manuscript. Hull, Quebec: University of Hull.

Rockefeller, Panel Reports. 1958. The pursuit of excellence; education and the future of America. Project report of the special studies project. Garden City, New York: Doubleday.

Rogers, A. H. 1958. The self-concept in paranoid schizophrenia. *Journal of Clinical Psychology* 14:365-366.

Rogers, C. R.

> 1942. *Counseling and psychotherapy.* Cambridge, Massachusetts: Houghton-Mifflin.

> 1947. The organization of personality. *Annals of Research Psychology* 2358-2368.

> 1951. *Client-centered therapy: its current practice, implications, and theory.* Boston: Houghton-Mifflin.

> 1959. A theory of therapy, personality, and interpersonal relationships as developed in a client-centered framework. In *Psychology: a study of science*, ed. S. Koch. New York: McGraw-Hill.

> 1969. *Freedom to learn: a view of what education might become.* Columbus, Ohio: Charles E. Merrill.

Rogers, C. R., and Dymond, R. F., eds. 1954. *Psychotherapy and personality change: co-ordinated studies in the client-centered approach.* Chicago: University of Chicago Press.

Rosen, B. C. 1956. The achievement syndrome: a psycho-cultural dimension of racial stratification. *American Sociology Review* 21:203-211.

Rosen, B. C., and Dandrade, R. 1961. The psychosocial origins of achievement motivation. *Sociometry* 51:203-207.

Rosen, E.

> 1956a. Self-appraisal and perceived desirability of MMPI personality traits. *Journal of Counseling Psychology* 3:44-51.

> 1956b. Self-appraisal, personal desirability, and perceived social desirability of personality traits. *Journal of Abnormal Social Psychology* 52:151-158.

Rosen, S., Levinger, C., and Lippitt, R. 1960. Desired change in self and others as a function of resource ownership. *Human Relations* 13:187-192.

Rosenberg, M.

> 1962a. Self-esteem and concern with public affairs. *Public Opinion Quarterly* 26:201-211.

> 1962b. The association between self-esteem and anxiety. *Psychological Review* 1:135-152.

> 1965. *Society and the adolescent self-image.* Princeton, New Jersey: Princeton University Press.

> 1968. Psychological selectivity in self-esteem formation. *The self in social interaction*, ed. C. Gordon and K. J. Gergen. New York: Wiley.

Roth, R. M. 1959. Role of self-concept in achievement. *Journal of Experimental Education* 27:265-281.

Rubenstein, E. A., and Lorr, M. A. 1956. Comparison of terminators and remainers in outpatient psychotherapy. *Journal of Clinical Psychology* 12:345-349.

Ruhly, V. M. 1971. A study of the relationship of self-concept, socioeconomic background, and psycholinguistic abilities to reading achievement of second-grade males residing in a suburban area. *Dissertation Abstracts* 31:4560-4563A.

Sampson, E. 1962. Birth order, need achievement, and conformity. *Journal of Abnormal Social Psychology* 64:155-159.

Sarason, Irvin, Gerald, 1966. *Personality: an objective approach.* New York: Wiley.

Scotland, W., and Hillner, M. L., Jr. 1962. Identification of defensiveness and self-esteem. *Dissertation Abstracts* 17:1 pp. 96-97.

Scott, W. A. 1958. Research definitions of mental health and mental illness. *Psychology Bulletin* 55:29-45.

Sears, P. S. 1941. Level of aspiration in relation to some variables of personality: clinical studies. *Journal of Social Psychology* 14:311-336.

Sears, P. S. 1963. Self-concept in the service of educational goals. *California Journal for Educational Improvement* 6:3-12.

Sears, P. S., and Sherman, W. 1964. *In pursuit of self-esteem.* Belmont, California: Wadsworth.

Sears, R. R. 1936. Experimental studies in projection, part 1: attribution of traits. *Journal of Social Psychology* 7:151-163.

Secord, P. F., and Jourard, S. M. 1953. The appraisal of body cathexis: body cathexis and the self. *Journal of Consulting Psychology* 17:343-347.

Seiden, R. H. 1966. Campus tragedy: a study of student suicide. *Journal of Abnormal Psychology* 71:389-399.

Sewell, W. H., and Shaw, V. P. 1968. Parents' educations and children's educational aspirations and achievements. *American Sociology Review* 33:2 pp. 191-209.

Sharma, S. L. 1956. Some personality correlates of changes in self-esteem under conditions of stress and support. *Journal of Education and Psychology* (Baroda) 14: 154-165.

Shavelson, R. J., Hubner, J. J., and Stanton, G. C. 1976. Self-concept validation of construct interpretations. *Review of Educational Research* 46:3 pp. 407-441.

Shaver, P. 1969. Measurement of the self-esteem and related constructs. In *Measures of social psychological attitudes*, ed. J. P. Robinson and P. B. Shoven. Ann Arbor: Michigan Institute for Social Research.

Shaw, M. C. 1960. Attitudes and child rearing practices of the parents of bright academic underachievers: a pilot study. Report on Research Project M-2843, supported by grant from National Institute of Health. Chico, California: Public Health Service; Chico State College.

Shaw, M. C. 1961. Need achievement scales as predictors of academic success. *Journal of Educational Psychology* 52:6 pp. 283-285.

Shaw, M. C., and Alvin, G. I. 1964. Self-concept of bright academic underachievers. *Personnel Guidance Journal* 42:401.

Shaw, M. C., and Block, M. D. 1960. The reaction to frustration of bright high school underachievers. *California Journal of Educational Research* 11:120-124.

Shaw, M. C., and Brown, B. T. 1957. Scholastic underachievement of bright college students. *Personnel Guidance Journal* 36: 195-199.

Shaw, M. C., and Cnubb, J. 1958. Hostility and able high school underachievers. *Journal of Counseling Psychology* 39:193-196.

Shaw, M. C., Edison, K., and Bell, H. M. 1960. The self-concepts of bright underachieving high school students as revealed by an objective checklist. *Personnel Guidance Journal* 39:193-196.

Shaw, M. C., and McEwan, J. T. 1960. The onset of academic underachievement in bright children. *Journal of Educational Psychology* 51:103-108.

Sheerer, E. T. 1949. An analysis of the relationship between acceptance of and respect for self and acceptance and respect for others in ten counseling cases. *Journal of Consulting Psychology* 13:169-175.

Sherman, M. 1949. Psychiatric insights into reading problems. In *Clinical studies in reading I*. Supplementary Educational Monographs, no. 68, pp. 130-132. Chicago: University of Chicago Press.

Sherwood, J. J. 1962. Self-identity and self-actualizations: a theory and research. Unpublished doctoral dissertation. Ann Arbor: University of Michigan.

Sherwood, J. J. 1965. Self-identity and referent others. *Sociometry* 28:66, 81.

Shoen, M. 1937. Human nature. In *Personality*, ed. G. W. Allport. New York: Holt.

Shostrum, E. 1966, 1968. *EITS manual for the personal orientation inventory*. San Diego, California: Educational Industrial Testing Service.

Siss, R. N. 1963. Expectations of mothers and teachers for independence and reading, and their influence upon reading and achievement and personality attributes of third-grade boys. *Dissertation Abstracts* 23:11 p. 4230.

Skemp, R. R. 1964. *Understanding mathematics*, Book 1. London: University of London Press.

Smith, C. P. 1969. *Achievement-related motives in children*. New York: Russell Sage Foundation.

Smith, D. F. 1971. A study of the relationship of teacher sex to fifth-grade boys' sex role preferences, general self-concept, and scholastic achievement in science and mathematics. *Dissertation Abstracts International* 31 (9-A): 4563.

Smith, D. M., Dokecki, P. R., and Davis, E. E. 1977. School-related factors influencing the self-concepts of children with learning problems. *Peabody Journal of Education* 54:185-195.

Smith, E. 1965. Significant differences between high ability achieving and nonachieving college freshmen as revealed by college data. *Journal of Educational Research* 59:10-12.

Smith, M. B. 1980. The phenomenological approach in personality theory: some critical remarks. *Journal of Abnormal Psychology* 45:516-522.

Smith, N. B. 1955. Research on reading and emotion. *School and Society* 1818-1890.

Snygg, D., and Combs, A. W. 1959. *Individual behavior: A perceptual approach to behavior*. New York: Harper and Row.

Snyder, J. W. 1969. A new use for SAT: helping salvage potential dropouts. *College Board Review* 70:5-9.

Soares, A., and Soares, L. 1965. Self-perceptions of culturally disadvantaged children. *American Educational Research Journal* 6:31-45.

Solley, C. M., and Stagner, R. 1956. Effects of magnitude of temporal barring type of goal and perceptions of self. *Journal of Experimental Psychology*.

Sorbin, R. R., and Jones, D. S. 1955. An experimental analysis of role behavior. *Journal of Abnormal Social Psychology* 51:236-241.

Sorbin, R. R., and Rosenberg, B. G. 1955. Contributions to role-taking theory, part 4: a method for obtaining a qualitative estimate of the self. *Journal of Social Psychology* 42:171-181.

Sorenson, G. 1967. *Toward an instructional model for counseling*. Los Angeles: Center for the Study of Evaluation of Instruction Progress.

Spache, G. D. 1957. Personality problems of retarded readers. *Journal of Educational Research* 50:461-469.

Stager, R. 1933. The relation of personality to academic aptitude and achievement. *Journal of Educational Research* 26:648-660.

Staines, J. W. 1958. The self-picture as a factor in the classroom. *British Journal of Educational Psychology* 18:97-111.

Steiner, I. D. 1957. Self-perception and goal-setting behavior. *Journal of Personal and Social Psychology* 57:344-355.

Stevenson, W. H. 1966. Monographs of the Society for Research in Child Development, nos. 5, 31. Chicago: University of Chicago Press.

Stoner, W. G. 1957. Factors related to the underachievement of high school students. *Dissertation Abstracts* 17:1 pp. 96-97.

Stottard, E., Thorley, S., Thoren, E., Cohen, A. R., and Zerder, A. 1957. The effects of group expectation and self-esteem upon self-evaluation. *Journal of Abnormal Social Psychology* 54:55-63.

Strodlbeck, F. L. 1955. Family interaction, values, and achievement. In *Talent society: new perspectives in the identification of talent*, ed. M. D. C. McClelland et al. Princeton, New Jersey: Van Nostrand.

Sullivan, H. S. 1947. *Conceptions of modern psychiatry*. Washington, D. C.: William Alanson White Psychiatric Foundation.

Sullivan, H. S. 1953. *The interpersonal theory of psychiatry*. New York: W. W. Norton.

Surbin, T. R. 1954. Role theory. In *Handbook of psychology*, ed. G. M. Sidzey. Cambridge, Massachusetts: Addison-Wesley.

Sutcliffe, C. 1958. Factors related to low achievement by high school pupils of high mental ability. Unpublished doctoral dissertation. Los Angeles: University of Southern California.

Sutton, R. 1961. An analysis of factors related to educational achievement. *Journal of Genetic Psychology* 98:193-201.

Svensson, N. 1962. Ability grouping and scholastic achievement. *Journal of Educational Research* 5:1 pp. 53-56.

Taylor, J. A. 1953. A personality scale of manifest anxiety. *Journal of Abnormal Social Psychology* 48:285-289.

Terman, L. M., and Oden, M. 1947. *The gifted child grows up*. Genetic Studies of Genius, no. 14. Stanford, California: Stanford University Press.

Thomas, J. B. 1973. *Self-concept in psychology and education: a review of research*. New York: Humanities Press.

Thomas, W. L. 1967. *The Thomas self-concept values test*. Rosemont, Illinois: Combined Motivation Systems.

Thomas, W. L. 1968. *The Thomas self-concept values test supplement*. Grand Rapids, Michigan: Educational Services Co.

Thompson, V. T. 1959. The relationship of self-acceptance to the consistency of employment of the vocationally rehabilitated. *Dissertation Abstracts* 19:2012-2013.

Thompson, W. 1972. *Correlates of the self-concept*. Nashville, Tennessee: Dede Wallace Center.

Toller, G. S. 1967. Certain aspects of the self-evaluations made by achieving and retarded readers of average and above-average intelligence. *Dissertation Abstracts International* 28 (3-A): 976.

Torrance, E. P.
> 1954a. Realizations about test performance as a function of self-concepts. *Journal of Social Psychology* 39:211-217.
> 1954b. Some practical uses of a knowledge of self-concepts in counseling and guid-

ance. *Educational Psychological Measurement* 14:120-127.

1962. Keeping creative talent alive. The *Times* Educational Supplement (London), no. 2462, p. 110 (July 27).

1963. *Education and the creative potential.* Minneapolis: University of Minneapolis Press.

Tyler, L. 1962. *Clinical psychology: introduction to research and practice.* New York: Appleton-Century-Crofts.

Typzkowa, M. 1968. Influence of family structure and school status. *Psychological Abstracts* 42:10 p. 15369.

Veroff, J., and Parker, B. 1960. An exploratory study of parental motives, parental attitudes, and social behavior of children. *Dissertation Abstracts* 20:3375-3376.

Videbeck, R. 1960. Self-conception and the reaction of others. *Sociometry* 22:351-35.

Wagonseller, B. R. 1972. A comparison of intellectual ability, achievement level, self-concept, and behavior problems exhibited by children labeled as learning disabled and emotionally disturbed. *Dissertation Abstracts* 32-5644A; 72-11:722.

Wahler, H. J. 1958. Social desirability and self-ratings of intakes, patients in treatment, and controls. *Journal of Consulting Psychology* 20:357-363.

Warren, H. S., and Carmichael, L. 1930. *Elements of human psychology.* Cited in Allport, G. W. 1937. *Personality*, p. 44. New York: Holt.

Warren, S. A., and Jannascone, L. L. 1959. Normal children who just don't try. *School Executive* 78:1 pp. 40-41.

Wattenberg, M. W., and Clifford, C. 1964. Relationships of self-concepts to beginning achievement in reading. *Child Development* 35:461-467.

Wedemeyer, C. A. 1953. Gifted achievers and nonachievers. *Journal of Higher Education* 24:25-30.

Weigard, G. 1957. Adaptiveness and the role of parents in academic success. *Personnel Guidance Journal* 35:5 pp. 518-522.

Wellington, C. B., and Wellington, J. 1965. *The underachievers: challenge and guidelines.* Chicago: Rand McNally.

Wessman, A. E., and Ricks, D. F. 1966. *Mood and personality.* New York: Holt, Rinehart, and Winston.

Wessman, A. E., Ricks, D. F., and Tyl, M. M. 1960. Characteristics and concomitants of mood fluctuation in college women. *Journal of Abnormal Social Psychology* 60: 117-126.

Westful, F. W. 1958. Selected variables in achievement or nonachievement of academically talented high school students. *Dissertation Abstracts* 18:389-392.

White, R. W. 1959. Motivation reconsidered: the concept of competence. *Psychology Review* 68:297-333.

Wiederholt, J. L. 1974. Historical perspectives on the education of the learning disabled. In *Journal of Special Education.* Philadelphia: JSE Press.

Williams, E. 1957. Selected cultural factors in scholastic achievement of a group of fifth-grade children in scranton public schools. *Dissertation Abstracts* 17:1 p. 288.

Williams, J. H. 1973. The relationship of self-concept and reading achievement in first-grade children. *Journal of Educational Research* 66:378-381.

Williams, M. S. 1958. Acceptance and performance among gifted elementary school children. *Educational Research Bulletin* 37:8 pp. 216-220.

Williams, R. L., and Cole, S. 1968. Self-concept and achievement. *Personnel Guidance Journal* 46:478-481.

Wilson, A. B. 1959. Residential segregation of social classes and aspirations of high school boys. *American Sociology Review* 24:6 pp. 836-845.

Wilson, R. C., and Morrow, W. R. 1962. School and career adjustment of bright high achieving and underachieving high school boys. *Journal of Genetic Psychology* 101:91-103.

Wing, S. W. 1966. A study of children whose reported self-concept differs from classmates' evaluation of them. Unpublished doctoral dissertation. Eugene, Oregon: University of Oregon.

Winterbottom, M. R. 1958. The relationship of need for achievement to learning experiences in independence and mastery. In *Motives in fantasy, action, and society*, ed. M. J. W. Atkinson, pp. 453-478. Princeton, New Jersey: Van Nostrand.

Witty, P. A. 1940. A genetic study of fifty gifted children. In *Intelligence, its nature and nurture*, 39th Yearbook of the National Society for the Study of Education, part 2, pp. 401-409. Bloominton, Illinois: Public School Publishing Co.

Wolpe, D. L. 1954. *America's resources of specialized talent.* New York: Harper.

Worchel, P. Adaptability screening of flying personnel: development of a self-concept inventory for predicting maladjustment. Report nos. 52-62. U.S. Air Force School of Aviation Medicine.

Wylie, R. 1961. *The self-concept.* Lincoln, Nebraska: University of Nebraska Press.

Yeudall, L. T. 1977. Neurophychological correlates of criminal psychopathology. Paper presented to the Fifth International Seminar in Comparative Clinical Criminology. Montreal, Canada.

Zahran, H. A. 1967. The self-concept in the psychological guidance of adolescents. *British Journal of Educational Psychology* 37:2 pp. 225-240.

Ziller, R., Hagner, J., Smith, M., and Long, B. 1969. Self-esteem: a self-social construct. *Journal of Consulting Psychology* 33:84-95.

Zimmer, H. 1954. Self-acceptance and its relation to conflict. *Journal of Consulting Psychology* 18:447-449.

Zimmer, H. 1956. Motivational factors in dyadic interaction. *Journal of Personal and Social Psychology* 24:251-261.

Zoolian, C. H. 1965. Factors related to differential achievement among boys in ninth-grade algebra. *Journal of Educational Research* 58:205-207.

Zuckerman, M., Baer, M., and Monashkin, I. 1956. Acceptance of self, parents, and people in patients and normals. *Journal of Clinical Psychology* 72:327-332.

Zuckerman, M., and Monashkin, I. 1957. Self-acceptance and psychopathology. *Journal of Consulting Psychology* 21:145-148.

SUBJECT INDEX

AUTHOR INDEX

ENHANCING